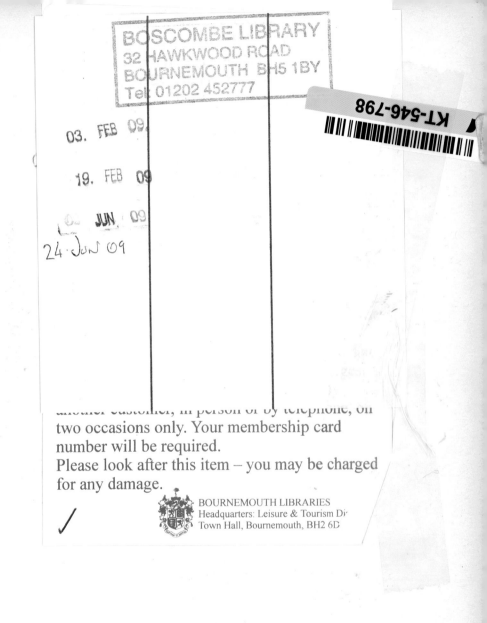

another customer, in person or by telephone, on
two occasions only. Your membership card
number will be required.
Please look after this item – you may be charged
for any damage.

WICKED
POEMS

EDITED BY ROGER McGOUGH

ILLUSTRATED BY NEAL LAYTON

BLOOMSBURY
CHILDREN'S
BOOKS

Research by Hilary McGough

With thanks to The Poetry Society

First published in Great Britain in 2002 by Bloomsbury Publishing Plc
38 Soho Square, London, W1D 3HB
This paperback edition first published in 2004

Individual poem details feature on the acknowledgements
page situated at the back of this book
Copyright © Text this selection Roger McGough 2002
Copyright © Illustrations Neal Layton 2002
The moral rights of the author and illustrator have been asserted

A CIP catalogue record of this book is available from the British Library
ISBN 0 7475 6195 8

Text design by Lobster Design

Printed in Great Britain by Clays Ltd, St Ives plc

10 9 8 7 6 5 4 3 2 1

All papers used by Bloomsbury Publishing are natural, recyclable products made
from wood grown in well-managed forests. The manufacturing processes
conform to the environmental regulations of the country of origin.

Contents

Big Wicked

Better be big wicked –
small wicked gets caught,
big wicked's a billion
small wicked's nought,

big wicked chews up a city
small wicked daubs on a wall,
big wicked gets portrait and statue
small wicked ends up in court,

big wicked has a bomb-proof Mercedes
small wicked TWOCs,*
big wicked steals a country
small wicked steals from shops,

better be big wicked
with bodyguards at your gate,
better not be small wicked
grassed-up by your mates.

HELEN DUNMORE

*Taking Without Owner's Consent = stealing cars

Don't Steal

Don't steal; thou'lt never then compete
Successfully in business. Cheat

AMBROSE BIERCE

Haiku

Like a boomerang,
mean words behind your friend's back
can come back to you.

MIKE JUBB

I Told a Lie Today

I told a lie today
and it curled up inside me
like a steel hard spring.

It was quite a clever lie,
no one guessed the truth,
they believed me.

But I've carried the twist of it
at the centre of my body, all day,
and I think it's expanding,
filling me up,
making my eyes feel red.

Perhaps it's going to uncoil suddenly
and burst me open,
showing everyone what I'm really like.

I think I had better confess,
before I'm completely unwound.

ROBIN MELLOR

Matilda

Who told Lies, and was Burned to Death

Matilda told such Dreadful Lies,
It made one Gasp and Stretch one's Eyes;
Her Aunt, who, from her Earliest Youth,
Had kept a Strict Regard for Truth,
Attempted to Believe Matilda:
The effort very nearly killed her,
And would have done so, had not She
Discovered this Infirmity.
For once, towards the Close of Day,
Matilda, growing tired of play,
And finding she was left alone,
Went tiptoe to the Telephone
And summoned the Immediate Aid
Of London's Noble Fire-Brigade.
Within an hour the Gallant Band
Were pouring in on every hand,
From Putney, Hackney Downs and Bow,
With Courage high and Hearts a-glow
They galloped, roaring through the Town,
'Matilda's House is Burning Down!'
Inspired by British Cheers and Loud
Proceeding from the Frenzied Crowd,
They ran their ladders through a score
Of windows on the Ball Room Floor;
And took Peculiar Pains to Souse
The Pictures up and down the House,

Until Matilda's Aunt succeeded
In showing them they were not needed
And even then she had to pay
To get the Men to go away!

It happened that a few Weeks later
Her Aunt was off to the Theatre
To see that Interesting Play
The Second Mrs. Tanqueray.
She had refused to take her Niece
To hear this Entertaining Piece:
A Deprivation Just and Wise
To Punish her for Telling Lies.
That Night a Fire did break out—
You should have heard Matilda Shout!
You should have heard her Scream and Bawl,
And throw the window up and call
To People passing in the Street—
(The rapidly increasing Heat
Encouraging her to obtain
Their confidence)—but all in vain!
For every time She shouted 'Fire!'
They only answered 'Little Liar!'
And therefore when her Aunt returned,
Matilda, and the House, were Burned.

HILAIRE BELLOC

Huff

I am in a tremendous huff—
Really, really bad.
It isn't any ordinary huff—
It's one of the best I've had.

I plan to keep it up for a month
Or maybe for a year
And you needn't think you can make me smile
Or talk to you. No fear.

I can do without you and her and them—
Too late to make amends.
I'll think deep thoughts on my own for a while,
Then find some better friends.

And they'll be wise and kind and good
And bright enough to see
That they should behave with proper respect
Towards somebody like me.

I do like being in a huff—
Cold fury is so heady.
I've been like this for half an hour
And it's cheered me up already.

Perhaps I'll give them another chance,
Now I'm feeling stronger
But they'd better watch out—my next big huff
Could last much, much, much longer.

WENDY COPE

I'm in a Rotten Mood

I'm in a rotten mood today,
a really rotten mood today,
I'm feeling cross,
I'm feeling mean,
I'm jumpy as a jumping bean,
I have an awful attitude—
I'M IN A ROTTEN MOOD!

I'm in a rotten mood today,
a really rotten mood today,
I'm in a snit,
I'm in a stew,
there's nothing that I care to do
but sit all by myself and brood—
I'M IN A ROTTEN MOOD!

I'm in a rotten mood today,
a really rotten mood today,
you'd better stay away from me,
I'm just a lump of misery,
I'm feeling absolutely rude—
I'M IN A ROTTEN MOOD!

JACK PRELUTSKY

As the Saying Goes . . .

'Sticks and stones
may break my bones
but words will never hurt me . . .'

like pig-face; smelly;
nerd-brain; slag;
like ugly witch
or bag or hag . . .

Sticks and stones
may miss my bones
and breaks, in time, will heal;
but words remain
as does the pain
their memory makes me feel:

. . . the saying never goes.

CELIA WARREN

Old Swear Word

An old swear word has been found
That few have ever heard,
Hidden in a box it was
A very naughty word.

On scraps of grubby paper
In marks of ancient ink,
A secret from another age
Returns to cause a stink.

They say it's so explosive
The army has been called,
A policeman who just looked in
Went absolutely bald.

If it was ever spoken
All switchboards would be jammed,
The government would argue
That such things should be banned.

But maybe they should save it
In case of World War Three,
A cheap and secret weapon
To beat the enemy.

If nuclear strikes were threatened
They'd open up the box,
And shout the horrid word out
Then everything would stop.

In a country far away
A million knees would knock,
As members of the public
Went reeling from the shock.

Faces would go hot and cold
And turn to greys and reds,
Eyes would open wide as doors
And pop from people's heads.

Dying of embarrassment
The enemy would flip,
For funny things can happen
When naughty words just slip.

STEVE TURNER

The Mobile Sting

There's Jacko, this kid in our class
And he's got a mobile, see?
Nice little yellow one.
And Cozzer hasn't got one.

So I get his number
And text him in Maths:
FanC a d8 Jacko?
And I sign it Phoebe,
Or rather FeeB
(That's Phoebe Boardman,
This really
Goodlooking girl in 4C).

And he texts back:
U bet! Where? When?
And I text him:
Sports shed. 4.
And he texts just two letters:
OK.

So that's Jacko hooked.
And at four o'clock
We're waiting for him,
Cozzer and me and Ted,
And he's on his own

Which is what we'd figured;
But the plan doesn't come off.
His nice little phone
Was confisc8ed in IT
For texting in lessons.

All the same
You should have seen Jacko's face
When he saw us three
Instead of the fabulous Phoebe.

He tried to run
But we caught him
And menaced him a bit,
About the flash yellow mobile,
And fancying Phoebe –
And left him to think about it.

GERARD BENSON

Lost on Level Seven

I'm playing on my Megadrive,
Don't ask me what it cost.
I'm up to Level Seven now,
But don't you know I'm lost?

    Disfigured ghouls and demons
    Are chasing after me,
    And a manic wrestler broke my back,
    Back on Level Three.

There's grizzly little gremlins
Down on Level One
That want to rip my heart out
Just for a bit of fun.

    There's a line of laughing lizards
    Down on Level Two
    Who seem to think my eyeballs
    Should be bubbling in their stew.

I told you about the wrestler
I met on Level Three.
It's true he snapped my vertebrae –
Now I'll never learn to ski.

    Level Four looked easy –
    Just a never-ending maze;
    Till it filled with gibbering goblins,
    Slobbering and crazed.

When I crawled in to Level Five,
I was just glad to be alive.
It's like a nightmare birthday party
With all your enemies invited –
   Here in the Megadrive.

   I'm losing all my energy –
   I need my Weetabix
   To beat the cloud of toxic gas
   That lurks on Level Six.

So here I am still sitting here,
Lost on Level Seven:
I started out at one o'clock,
And now it's gone eleven.

   I don't hear you say it's teatime;
   I don't know my mates have knocked.
   I'm stuck inside this Megadrive
   With all the exits blocked.

Now you know the reason
That I just can't hear you –
I've turned into a zombie,
And now I'm turning blue!

        DAVE WARD

Eddy Scott Goes Out to Play

Outside, the street is dark with rain,
The arcade is brightly lit with screens;
Eddy feeds his dinner money
To hypnotising fruit machines.

'Don't get into trouble,
Don't talk to funny men,
Here's two pounds to buy your dinner.'
Eddy's left alone again.

The coins clunk down, the fruit rolls round
The bright lights flash like mad,
Then disappear like the dinner
Eddy hasn't had.

Eddy's mum's at work all day,
Eddy's dad has gone away,
Hot or cold, wet or fine,
Eddy Scott's sent out to play.

The money's gone. No food to eat.
Eddy checks round all the trays
In case somebody's missed a coin.
'No money, sonny?' someone says.

'Don't get into trouble,
Don't talk to funny men,
Here's two pounds to buy your dinner.'
Eddy's left alone again.

'I'll lend you money if you like,
Or how about some sweets?
I've seen you here and there before,
Wandering round the streets.'

Eddy's mum's at work all day,
Eddy's dad has gone away,
Hot or cold, wet or fine,
Eddy Scott's sent out to play.

'Would you like a slap-up meal?
You would? Get in the car,
I'll take you to a place I know
It isn't very far.'

'Don't get into trouble,
Don't talk to funny men,
Here's two pounds to buy your dinner.'
Eddy's left alone again.

Mum gets home at six o'clock,
'Eddy, are you home?' she'll call.
There'll be no answer, just her voice
Echoing along the hall.

Eddy's mum's at work all day,
Eddy's dad has gone away,
Hot or cold, wet or fine,
Eddy was sent out to play.

DAVID ORME

No Rest for the Wicked

Little minor wickednesses:
Drumming your fingers while eating your porridge
Thinking of Christmas twice on a Tuesday
Spreading the front door with Marmite or butter
Tickling your sister in a Teletubbies outfit
No rest for the wicked

Greater wickednesses:
Blowing your nose while watching the telly
Counting to thirty while thinking of twenty
Smiling at nothing at the checkout in Tesco's
Uttering curses in Spanish in Greenland
No rest for the wicked

Wickednesses to take seriously:
Cheating at chess in an unbuttoned cardigan
Stealing a moment before three in the afternoon
Killing time slowly while biting your nails
Dreaming while spitting and doing the opposite
No rest for the wicked

Wickedness beyond all forgiveness:
Running backwards not looking where you've been
Staring at spaces where nobody goes
Lying while standing, standing while lying
Resting when wicked, being wicked when resting
No rest for the wicked

GEORGE SZIRTES

The Dream-Stealers

Keep very still.
Don't turn. Don't look.
It's just a tube.
It's just a hook.

It needn't hurt.
Don't try to scream.
It's just a hook.
It's just a dream.

It's just a dream
We're taking out.
Don't try to scream.
Don't try to shout.

Forget the words,
The things they said.
It's just a dream.
It's in your head.

Inhale the gas.
Keep breathing in.
You'll barely feel
The breaking skin.

The barest jab.
The merest twist.
A dream you've lost
Is never missed.

Just like before.
Just like last night.
Was that so bad?
Don't try to fight.

It's just your dreams.
We'll dig them out.
Don't try to move.
Don't try to shout.

Here comes the gas.
You hear the hiss.
You'll wake. You won't
Remember this.

DAVID BATEMAN

Hunger

I come among the peoples like a shadow.
I sit down by each man's side.

None sees me, but they look on one another,
And know that I am there.

My silence is like the silence of the tide
That buries the playground of children;

Like the deepening of frost in the slow night,
When birds are dead in the morning.

Armies trample, invade, destroy,
With guns roaring from earth and air.

I am more terrible than armies,
I am more feared than the cannon.

Kings and chancellors give commands;
I give no command to any;

But I am listened to more than kings
And more than passionate orators.

I unswear words, and undo deeds.
Naked things know me.

I am first and last to be felt of the living.
I am Hunger.

LAURENCE BINYON

22

The Deserted Village

We came over the mountain
And found a village of secrets.

A street, a church, a school,
A village green.
But all we could hear was silence.
No children, no people,
No bleating of sheep on the hills
Or cackle of rooks in the trees,
No bells from the church.

No smoke from the chimneys
And the windows were watching eyes.
We crept closer and peered in
And saw that the rooms were bare
No food on the tables,
No fires in the hearths.

There were seats on the green
But where were the old folk with stories to tell
And where were the children with games to play?
Or the wives and the fathers, where were they?

We wanted to shout out and shatter the silence
But it clutched at our tongues,
It clutched at our hearts
And we walked on into the darkening day
And down to the valley, miles away.

BERLIE DOHERTY

Ghost Town

From the back-streets down by the aqueduct
Come the undead ones with their blood all sucked.
They've a dreadful smell. They don't look well.
Their souls are sold to him from Hell.
They've grown stone-cold and their eyes are glazed.
When they sense warm flesh they become half-crazed.
They're just like something from a horror movie.
If they weren't so real, they'd be really groovy.

They're dead but they won't lie down.
They're dead but they won't lie down.
They're in our town and they're walking round.
They're dead but they won't lie down.

Wherever we go, they're in hot pursuit,
So we stab, we shoot, we electrocute
To no avail. Though, God knows why,
They refuse point-blank to properly die.
We can't even go to the supermarket.
They crowd round the car when we try to park it.
The dog got out and can't be found,
Though we can hear it howling underground.

They're dead but they won't lie down.
They're dead but they won't lie down.
They're in our town and they're walking round.
They're dead but they won't lie down.

Their clothes are lousy, their complexions vile.
They're the walking weird. They've got no style.
They're out all night with their clanking chains.
They eat eyeballs whole and they suck out brains.
And we can't now phone cos they've cut the wires.
And they've crashed the car and slashed the tyres.
And we can't relax cos of all the screams.
When we finally sleep, they invade our dreams.

They're dead but they won't lie down.
They're dead but they won't lie down.
They're in our town and they're walking round.
They're dead but they won't lie down.

There's a demon in the attic. In the cellar there's a ghoul.
And there's something in the bathroom that's decidedly uncool.
And you don't look too good. Are those maggots in your hair?
And I'm staring in the mirror, but my reflection isn't there.

We're dead but we won't lie down.
We're dead but we won't lie down.
We're in your town and we're walking round.
We're dead but we won't lie down.

NICK TOCZEK

The Evil Doctor
Mucus Spleen

Who schemes an evil scheming scheme?
Who dreams an evil dreaming dream?
Who wants to rule the world supreme?
Who has the evillest inventions?
Who has the evillest intentions?
Thoughts and plans too dark to mention . . .
The Evil Evil Evil . . . it's Doctor Mucus Spleen!

Who's the crime at every scene?
Who wants to turn the whole world green?
Who's not ozone friendly-clean?
His phaser laser quasar blaster
Blasts his poison ever faster
Emerald phlegm in quick dry plaster
The Evil Evil Evil . . . it's Doctor Mucus Spleen.

Whose operations and routines
Take science to the dark extremes?
Who's part alien, part machine . . .
His cauldrons bubble, test tubes fizz.
Sockets hum and wires whizz
I bet you know just who it is . . .
The Evil Evil Evil . . . it's Doctor Mucus Spleen.

Whose habits are the most obscene?
Whose toes are full of jam between?
Whose armpits boil and trousers steam?
Who drips slime and goo and ooze?
Who smells of ancient sweat stained shoes?
Who's the baddest of bad news . . .
The Evil Evil Evil . . . it's Doctor Mucus Spleen.

Whose underpants are trampolines?
Whose eyes are like two tangerines?
Whose skin's like rotten clotted cream?
Who has the stench of used baked beans?
Who makes your eyes and nostrils stream?
Who needs total quarantine?
The Evil Evil Evil . . . it's Doctor Mucus Spleen.

He's mean! He's green! He'll make you scream!
The baddest villain ever seen!
Watch out for his laser beam!
The Evil Evil Evil Evil Doctor Mucus Spleen!

PAUL COOKSON

Scarecrow

the scarecrow
looks sad tonight all covered in rags
her solitude made of sticks
flapping in the dark field
and her eyes that won't shut
watching the cows at sleep.
with no shoes
and wind in her pockets,
she counts those stars
she can see
from her fixed angle
and listens to the black sticks rubbing
as she spits her curses at the moon.

STEF PIXNER

Hallowe'en

This is the night when witches fly
On their whizzing broomsticks through the wintry sky;
Steering up the pathway where the stars are strewn,
They stretch skinny fingers to the waking moon.

This is the night when old wives tell,
Strange and creepy stories, tales of charm and spell;
Peering at the pictures flaming in the fire
They wait for whispers from a ghostly choir.

This is the night when angels go
In and out the houses, winging o'er the snow;
Clearing out the demons from the countryside
They make it new and ready for Christmastide.

LEONARD CLARK

Witches' Chant

Round about the cauldron go:
In the poisoned entrails throw.
Toad, that under cold stone
Days and nights has thirty-one
Sweated venom sleeping got,
Boil thou first in the charmèd pot.
    Double, double toil and trouble;
    Fire burn and cauldron bubble.

Fillet of a fenny snake,
In the cauldron boil and bake;
Eye of newt and toe of frog,
Wool of bat and tongue of dog,
Adder's fork and blindworm's sting,
Lizard's leg and owlet's wing.
For a charm of powerful trouble,
Like a hell-broth boil and bubble.
    Double, double toil and trouble;
    Fire burn and cauldron bubble.

Scale of dragon, tooth of wolf,
Witch's mummy, maw and gulf
Of the ravenous salt-sea shark,
Root of hemlock digged in the dark,
Make the gruel thick and slab:
Add thereto a tiger's chaudron,
For the ingredients of our cauldron.
  Double, double toil and trouble,
  Fire burn and cauldron bubble.

from *Macbeth*,
WILLIAM SHAKESPEARE

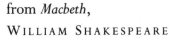

In the Green Wood

'Here in my cottage
deep in the green wood
I live on my own
and eat children pud.
No one would guess
that I'm up to no good
here in my cottage
deep in the green wood.

'I stand at the door
and look pretty nice.
My lipstick is red,
my eyes green as ice,
and my cottage is made
of sugar and spice
with caramel cats
and marzipan mice.

'Kids lost in the wood
stop off here to eat.
My windows and walls
they find such a treat.
They think that I'm ace
and terribly sweet
when I ask them inside
to rest their poor feet.

'As soon as they're trapped
I bolt the front door.
The shocked kids see bones
all over the floor.
They see I'm a witch
with warts on her jaw,
one broken brown tooth
and wig made of straw.

'The kids try to hide
in my smelly old room
but I soon sniff them out
in the cobwebby gloom.
I give them a whack
with a dirty great broom
and into my oven
they go to their doom.

'I bake the lost kids
till they're tender and nice
then serve them up hot
with lashings of rice.
I garnish with gnats
and finely ground lice
here in my cottage
of (hah!) sugar and spice.

'Parents come searching
– just as they should,
but none of them guess
I'm up to no good
or that their lost kids
are yum scrummy pud
here in my cottage
deep in the green wood.'

WES MAGEE

Nanny Neverley

Old Nanny Neverley
came from Back There.
She sat in the sunshine
with frost in her hair.
I'm going home soon, she said.
Never said where.

Sweet crumbly biscuits,
ghostly-grey tea
and a smile would be waiting.
She listened to me
and sometimes to someone else
I couldn't see

and when we fell silent
and couldn't say why
she glanced at the window.
She smiled at the sky.
Look There, you missed it.
An angel went by.

It was one of her stories,
like: *I'm growing too;*
you grow up, I grow down . . .
She told lies, I knew.
Only, now that she's gone
nothing else seems quite true.

PHILIP GROSS

35

The Last Witch in Nantwich

Her eyes are black. She owns a broom.
I've seen her in a pointy hat.
I found a witch-knot in her room,
And sometimes, in the evening gloom,
When corners fade, and shadows bloom,
I've caught her talking to the cat.

My mum's a witch, I should have guessed
That morning, when I found the toad.
It looked a bit like Mr Best
Who used to live across the road.

The kids were all afraid of him,
But now, they say, he's gone for good,
He used to argue with my mum
He never really understood.

My mum's a witch, a wicked witch,
I've seen her in that pointy hat.
On moonlit nights, she rides a broom,
She keeps a witch-knot in her room,
And last night, in the evening gloom,
When corners fade, and shadows bloom,
I caught her talking to the cat.

JOHN BURNSIDE

36

Unstable Mabel

Mabel's unstable, be careful, beware
Of that look in her eyes that says, 'I don't care.
I'll do what I want, however unfair.'
Mabel's unstable, and isn't all there.
Mabel's unstable, and able I'm sure
To nail up an angel on to the back door.
Somebody must take her far, far away.
That's what we long for, and pray for each day.
No one remembers from where Mabel came.
Found on the doorstep and brought in from the rain
She sat in a corner, glowered and moaned,
'I was raised by a man whose head was horned.'
Mabel's unstable and if you want proof
Look down at her foot. You'll find only a hoof.
Her eyes are ablaze, like cinders, like fire,
And her dark hair is tangled like razor-sharp wire.

BRIAN PATTEN

The Stones

Worried mothers bawled her name
To call wild children from their games.

'Nellie Mulcahy! Nellie Mulcahy!
If ye don't come home,
She'll carry ye off in her big black bag.'

Her name was fear and fear begat obedience,
But one day she made a real appearance –
A harmless hag with a bag on her back.
When the children heard, they gathered together
And in a trice were
Stalking the little weary traveller –
Ten, twenty, thirty, forty.
Numbers gave them courage
Though, had they known it,
Nellie was more timid by far
Than the timidest there.
Once or twice she turned to look
At the bravado-swollen pack.
Slowly the chant began –

'Nellie Mulcahy! Nellie Mulcahy!
Wicked old woman! Wicked old woman!'

One child threw a stone.
Another did likewise.
Soon the little monsters
Were furiously stoning her

Whose name was fear.
When she fell bleeding to the ground,
Whimpering like a beaten pup,
Even then they didn't give up,
But pelted her like mad.
Suddenly they stopped, looked at
Each other, then at Nellie, lying
On the ground, shivering.

Slowly they withdrew
One by one.

Silence. Silence.
All the stones were thrown.

Between the hedges of their guilt
Cain-children shambled home.

Alone,
She dragged herself up,
Crying in small half-uttered moans,
Limped away across the land,
Black bag on her back,
Agony racking her bones.

Between her and the children,
Like hideous forms of fear —
The stones.

BRENDAN KENNELLY

Mrs Dungeon Brae

Mrs Dungeon Brae lived on the Isle of Mull,
the fairest of the rarest,
of all the western isles,
in a ramshackle farm house,
close to the hoarse, heaving sea.

Every morning Mrs Dungeon Brae
was up with her white goats
pulling their teats for thin milk.
If she stumbled across a stranger
on her acre of land,

She reached for her gun, an old
long gun that belonged to her father,
his father before him, his father before him.
Then fired in the fern-scented air;
and watched the crows and stranger scatter.

She laughed a grim dry cough of a laugh.
Her face had all of Scotland's misery —
every battle fought and lost;
but her cheeks were surprises — a dash
of colour, a sprig of purple heather

peeping over the barren hillside.
Once, alone, in her house,
she sat down in her armchair
with her grey hair yanked into a bun
and died –

A tight, round ball of a death.
And nobody found her:
every body was terrified of trespassing.
So the skeleton of Mrs Dungeon Brae
sits on her favoured armchair,

And the radio is playing Bach.
Ach. Ach.
Mrs Dungeon Brae.
The strings haunting the bones of Mrs Dungeon Brae.
Ach. Ach. Mrs Dungeon Brae. Ach. Ach.

JACKIE KAY

Jamjar

A girl in her garden peeped into a jamjar and fell inside.
She passed a wasp as she fell, it was licking
a smear of strawberry jam from the rim of the jar.
How far is the bottom? she cried as she fell.
Far, very far, drawled the wasp, *terribly far*.

Down she fell. The jar was a bell and her scream
was its tinkly, echoing ring. A green caterpillar
crawled up the outside glass of the jar, blinked
with its bulging alien eyes. *Help!* screeched the girl. *Help!*
Alas, it lisped, *there's no help in the whole wide world*.

On she hurled, into the well of the jar, till the opening
was a tiny star and dandelion-clocks were silver planets
spinning in space. A spider hung from a thread
and peered at her face. *Throw me a rope!* she begged.
Not here, not now, it sneered, *nor any time or place*.

Bump. The jamjar's floor was snow and ice, stretching
for freezing miles. The girl skated away, all alone,
calling for home. White wolves ran in her tracks
under the hard stars. *Show me the way*, she sobbed.
No way to show, they howled, *and no way back*.

Then a hand picked up the jar; a mean squint eye swam
like a needlefish to the glass; poisonous breath clouded it over.
This will do for a vase, said a spiteful voice, as a Witch
filled up the jamjar with water, then stared in amazed,
glee in her eyes, at her swimming and brand-new creature.

CAROL ANN DUFFY

Alternative Endings
to an Unwritten Ballad

I stole through the dungeons, while everyone slept,
    Till I came to the cage where the Monster was kept.
There, locked in the arms of a Giant Baboon,
    Rigid and smiling, lay . . . MRS RAVOON!

I climbed the clock tower in the first morning sun
    And 'twas midday at least 'ere my journey was done;
But the clock never sounded the last stroke of noon,
    For there, from the clapper, swung MRS RAVOON!

I hauled in the line, and I took my first look
    At the half-eaten horror that hung from the hook.
I had dragged from the depths of the limpid lagoon
    The luminous body of MRS RAVOON.

I fled in the storm, the lightning and thunder,
    And there, as a flash split the darkness asunder,
Chewing a rat's-tail and mumbling a rune,
    Mad in the moat squatted MRS RAVOON!

I stood by the waters so green and so thick,
    And I stirred at the scum with my old, withered stick;
When there rose through the ooze, like a monstrous balloon,
    The bloated cadaver of MRS RAVOON.

Facing the fens, I looked back from the shore
  Where all had been empty a moment before;
And there by the light of the Lincolnshire moon,
  Immense on the marshes, stood . . . MRS RAVOON!

PAUL DEHN

White Ones

with small scritchety claws
and pink
shortsighted blink
ing-in-the-sunlight
eyes that looked raw
as if they'd cried all night . . .

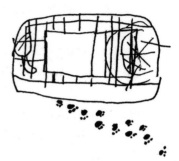

One morning they were gone.

On holiday,
Dad says. *Gone to stay*
with their friends
in the pet shop. And so I pretend
I don't know about the cage door
he left open. I try to ignore

the look on the face of the cat.

It isn't that
wakes me up in the darkness. No,
it's the scritch and the scratch
at the bars, the pink-eyed
lies. They're only little
white ones, oh

but watch them breed and grow.

PHILIP GROSS

By the Pricking of My Thumbs . . .

By the pricking of my thumbs
Something wicked this way comes

By the parings of my nails
Here's a creature with two tails

By the snippings of my hair
I think I see a grizzly bear

By the blinking of my eye
I heard a spider catch a fly

By the doffing of my hat
My shadow's turned into a bat . . .

By the cold draughts in my room
My mother rode off on her broom.

By the dripping of my nose
I know something no-one knows . . .

By the itching of my palm
I wonder if . . . Stay calm, stay calm.

GEORGE SZIRTES

Lazy Witch

Lazy witch,
What's wrong with you?
   Get up and stir your magic brew.
   Here's candlelight to chase the gloom.
   Jump up and mount your flying broom
   And muster up your charms and spells
   And wicked grins and piercing yells.
   It's Halloween! There's work to do!
Lazy witch,
What's wrong with you?

MYRA COHN LIVINGSTON

The Wind in a Frolic

The wind one morning sprung up from sleep,
Saying, 'Now for a frolic! now for a leap!
Now for a mad-cap, galloping chase!
I'll make a commotion in every place!'
So it swept with a bustle right through a great town,
Creaking the signs, and scattering down
Shutters; and whisking, with merciless squalls,
Old women's bonnets and gingerbread stalls.
There never was heard a much lustier shout,
As the apples and oranges trundled about;
And the urchins, that stand with their thievish eyes
For ever on watch, ran off each with a prize.

Then away to the field it went blustering and humming,
And the cattle all wondered whatever was coming;
It plucked by their tails the grave, matronly cows,
And tossed the colts' manes all about their brows,
Till, offended at such a familiar salute,
They all turned their backs, and stood sullenly mute.
So on it went, capering and playing its pranks:
Whistling with reeds on the broad river's banks;
Puffing the birds as they sat on the spray,
Or the traveller grave on the king's highway.
It was not too nice to hustle the bags
Of the beggar, and flutter his dirty rags:
'Twas so bold, that it feared not to play its joke
With the doctor's wig, or the gentleman's cloak.

Through the forest it roared, and cried gaily, 'Now,
You sturdy old oaks, I'll make you bow!'
And it made them bow without more ado,
Or it cracked their great branches through and through.
Then it rushed like a monster on cottage and farm,
Striking their dwellers with sudden alarm;
And they ran out like bees in a midsummer swarm.
There were dames with their 'kerchiefs tied over their caps,
To see if their poultry were free from mishaps;
The turkeys they gobbled, the geese screamed aloud,
And the hens crept to roost in a terrified crowd;
There was rearing of ladders, and logs laying on
Where the thatch from the roof threatened soon to be gone.

But the wind had passed on, and had met in a lane,
With a schoolboy, who panted and struggled in vain;
For it tossed him, and twirled him, then passed, and he stood,
With his hat in a pool, and his shoe in the mud.

There was a poor man, hoary and old,
Cutting the heath on the open wold—
The strokes of his bill were faint and few,
Ere this frolicsome wind upon him blew;
But behind him, before him, about him it came,
And the breath seemed gone from his feeble frame;
So he sat him down with a muttering tone,
Saying, 'Plague on the wind! was the like ever known?
But nowadays every wind that blows
Tells one how weak an old man grows!'

But away went the wind in its holiday glee;
And now it was far on the billowy sea,
And the lordly ships felt its staggering blow,
And the little boats darted to and fro,
But lo! it was night, and it sank to rest,
On the sea-bird's rock, in the gleaming west,
Laughing to think, in its fearful fun,
How little of mischief it had done.

WILLIAM HOWITT

Child on Top of a Greenhouse

The wind billowing out the seat of my britches,
My feet crackling splinters of glass and dried putty,
The half-grown chrysanthemums staring up like accusers,
Up through the streaked glass, flashing with sunlight,
A few white clouds all rushing eastward,
A line of elms plunging and tossing like horses,
And everyone, everyone pointing up and shouting!

THEODORE ROETHKE

To Fly . . .

Head down
Run faster
Suddenly barefoot
Run faster
Pass yourself gasping
Run faster
Brush off your shadow
Run faster
Then flick back your heels
Aim your chin at the Moon
And leap-frog the sky . . .

KEVIN McCANN

53

Flight of the Roller-Coaster

Once more around should do it, the man confided . . .

and, sure enough, when the roller-coaster reached the peak
of the giant curve above me, screech of its wheels
almost drowned out by the shriller cries of the riders,

instead of the dip and plunge with its landslide of screams,
it rose in the air like a movieland magic carpet,
   some wonderful bird,

and without fuss or fanfare swooped slowly across
   the amusement-park,
over Spook's Castle, ice-cream booths, shooting-gallery.
   And losing no height

made the last yards above the beach, where the cucumber-cool
brakeman in the last seat saluted
a lady about to change from her bathing-suit.

Then, as many witnesses reported, headed leisurely
   out over the water,
disappearing all too soon behind a low-flying flight of clouds.

RAYMOND SOUSTER

Like Rollerblades

Like rollerblades, we make a pair
Watch us practise; with such flair
Pavements fly beneath our feet
In this kingdom of concrete
The original polyurethane pals
Surfing down suburban hills
Gossip, giggle, God it's great
To hang out with my best mate.

But my best mate's become a spy,
Sold my secrets. I blink my eye
And he has gone to the other side.
The Gang ride by; I try to hide,
Cover my feelings with concrete
As pavements fly beneath my feet
I climb the hills of hurt and hate
To get away from my best mate.

ANDREW FUSEK PETERS

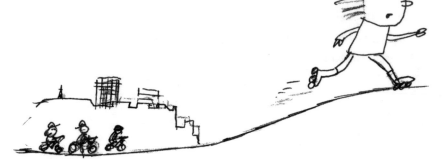

Brother and Sister

'Sister, sister go to bed!
Go and rest your weary head.'
Thus the prudent brother said.

'Do you want a battered hide,
Or scratches to your face applied?'
Thus his sister calm replied.

'Sister, do not raise my wrath.
I'd make you into mutton broth
As easily as kill a moth!'

The sister raised her beaming eye
And looked on him indignantly
And sternly answered, 'Only try!'

Off to the cook he quickly ran.
'Dear Cook, please lend a frying-pan
To me as quickly as you can.'

'And wherefore should I lend it you?'
'The reason, Cook, is plain to view.
I wish to make an Irish stew.'

'What meat is in that stew to go?'
'My sister'll be the contents!'
                    'Oh!'
'You'll lend the pan to me, Cook?'
                    'No!'

Moral: Never stew your sister.

LEWIS CARROLL

Sometimes

Sometimes I share things,
And everyone says
'Isn't it lovely? Isn't it fine?'

I give my little brother
Half my ice-cream cone
And let him play
With toys that are mine.

But today
I don't feel like sharing.
Today
I want to be let alone.
Today
I don't want to give my little brother
A single thing except
A shove.

EVE MERRIAM

Cradle Song

Little baby sister,
Fast asleep.
If I were to poke you,
Would you weep?

If I were to pinch you,
Would you yell?
Mummy wouldn't like that –
She'd give me hell.

No, I will not harm you,
Do not cry.
Darling little baby,
Hushabye.

Lulla, lulla, rock you.
What a din!
Darling little baby,
Pack it in.

Could you please stop bawling,
Just for me?
This lullaby's a failure,
I can see.

I'll be in big trouble,
Thanks to you.
Little baby sister,
Lullaboo!

WENDY COPE

Dave Dirt's Christmas Presents

Dave Dirt wrapped his Christmas presents
Late on Christmas Eve
And gave his near relations things
That you would not believe.

His brother got an Odour-Eater –
Second-hand one, natch.
For Dad he chose, inside its box,
A single burnt-out match.

His sister copped the sweepings from
His hairy bedroom rug,
While Mum received a centipede
And Granny got a slug.

Next day he had the nerve to sit
Beneath the Christmas tree
And say: 'OK, I've done my bit –
What have you got for me?'

KIT WRIGHT

60

A Song About Myself

There was a naughty boy
  And a naughty boy was he
He ran away to Scotland
  The people for to see—
    There he found
    That the ground
    Was as hard
    That a yard
    Was as long,
    That a song
    Was as merry,
    That a cherry
    Was as red—
    That lead
    Was as weighty
    That forescore
    Was as eighty
    That a door
    Was as wooden
    As in England—
    So he stood in
    His shoes
    And he wonder'd
    He stood in his
    Shoes and he wonder'd.

JOHN KEATS

61

Don't-Care Didn't Care

Don't-care didn't care;
   Don't-care was wild.
Don't-care stole plum and pear
   Like any beggar's child.

Don't-care was made to care,
   Don't-care was hung:
Don't-care was put in the pot
   And boiled till he was done.

TRADITIONAL

Mama, Mama

Mama, Mama, oh what is this
That looks like strawberry jam?
Hush, Hush, my dear, 'tis poor Papa
Run over by a tram.

HARRY GRAHAM

Tender-Heartedness

Billy, in one of his nice new sashes,
Fell in the fire and was burnt to ashes;
Now, although the room grows chilly,
I haven't the heart to poke poor Billy.

HARRY GRAHAM

The Adventures of Isabel

Isabel met an enormous bear,
Isabel, Isabel, didn't care;
The bear was hungry, the bear was ravenous,
The bear's big mouth was cruel and cavernous.
The bear said, Isabel, glad to meet you,
How do, Isabel, now I'll eat you!
Isabel, Isabel, didn't worry,
Isabel didn't scream or scurry,
She washed her hands and she straightened her hair up,
Then Isabel quietly ate the bear up.

Once in a night as black as pitch
Isabel met a wicked witch.
The witch's face was cross and wrinkled,
The witch's gums with teeth were sprinkled.
Ho ho, Isabel! the old witch crowed,
I'll turn you into an ugly toad!
Isabel, Isabel, didn't worry,
Isabel didn't scream or scurry,
She showed no rage, she showed no rancor,
But she turned the witch into milk
                    and drank her.

Isabel once was asleep in bed
When a horrible dream crawled into her head.
It was worse than a dinosaur, worse than a shark,
Worse than an octopus oozing in the dark.
'Boo!' said the dream, with a dreadful grin,
'I'm going to scare you out of your skin!'
Isabel, Isabel, didn't worry,
Isabel didn't scream or scurry,
Isabel had a cleverer scheme;
She just woke up and fooled that dream.

OGDEN NASH

Fair Play

Mirror mirror on the wall
Could you please return our ball
Our football went through your crack
You have two now
Give one back.

BENJAMIN ZEPHANIAH

Prayer of the Selfish Child

Now I lay me down to sleep,
I pray the Lord my soul to keep,
And if I die before I wake,
I pray the Lord my toys to break.
So none of the other kids can use 'em . . .
Amen.

SHEL SILVERSTEIN

Homework

Bash the cymbals
and the drums
brush the chimes
I've done my sums

Close the curtains
dim the light
go to bed
not one is right

STEWART HENDERSON

The Cane

The teacher
had some thin springy sticks
for making kites.

Reminds me
of the old days, he said;
and swished one.

The children
near his desk laughed nervously,
and pushed closer.

A cheeky girl
held out her cheeky hand.
Go on, Sir!

said her friends.
Give her the stick, she's always
playing up!

The teacher
paused, then did as he was told.
Just a tap.

Oh, Sir!
We're going to tell on you,
The children said.

Other children
left their seats and crowded round
the teacher's desk.

Other hands
went out. Making kites was soon
forgotten.

My turn next!
He's had one go already!
That's not fair!

Soon the teacher,
to save himself from the crush,
called a halt.

(It was
either that or use the cane
for real.)

Reluctantly,
the children did as they were told
and sat down.

If you behave
yourselves, the teacher said,
I'll cane you later.

ALLAN AHLBERG

Bad Report – Good Manners

My daddy said, 'My son, my son,
This school report is bad.'
I said, 'I did my best I did,
My dad my dad my dad.'

'Explain, my son, my son,' he said,
'Why *bottom* of the class?'
'I stood aside, my dad my dad,
To let the others pass.'

SPIKE MILLIGAN

Play No Ball

What a wall!
Play No ball,
It tells us all.
Play No Ball,
　By Order!

Lick no lolly.
Skip no rope.
Nurse no dolly.
Wish no hope.
Hop no scotch.
Ring no bell.
Telly no watch.
Joke no tell.

Tyre no pump.
Down no fall.
Up no jump.
Name no call.
　And . . .
Play No Ball.
No Ball. No Ball.
　BY ORDER!

GERARD BENSON

It wasn't me

It wasn't me,
believe me.
I never did,
I wouldn't dare.
It couldn't be,
believe me.
I don't know who,
I swear.

It never was,
believe me.
I wouldn't dream . . .
I swear.
You think who did it
could have climbed up
on the
bathroom chair?

The cabinet is open?
But I didn't,
please,
I swear.
I know it's
really naughty.
Could it be
the new au pair?

And the hamster's
wearing lipstick
and there's perfume
on his fur?
It wasn't me,
believe me.
I don't know who,
I swear.

STEWART HENDERSON

My Furry Feet

I am a well-conducted child,
Not disobedient or wild
But marvellously meek and mild
   And very clean and neat.
What wicked person left a pair
Of muddy footprints on the chair?
Don't look at me. I wasn't there.
   It was my furry feet.

I eat my cake and drop no crumbs.
I am especially good at sums.
I am a superstar with mums.
   Old ladies call me sweet.
Who tripped poor Piers ffitzparker-ffitch
And laid him in a muddy ditch?
I know the criminals – by which
   I mean my furry feet.

Some children howl like wolves, or feast
Like hogs, or stomp like wildebeest.
I am not like them in the least
   But quiet and discreet.
Who booted Angie's B – U – M,
A horrid deed we all condemn?
It wasn't me. 'Cos it was them.
   My dreadful furry feet.

Nobody is as nice as me,
From top to well below the knee
I am as perfect as can be,
    And good enough to eat.
So, though the evidence is strong,
Remember – I can do no wrong.
This is the chorus of my song.
    IT WAS MY FURRY FEET!

JOHN WHITWORTH

Tongue-Twister

Watch out for the dreaded Tongue-twister
When he pulls on his surgical gloves.
Keep your eyes open, your mouth tightly shut,
Twisting tongues is the thing that he loves.

It's the slippery, squirmy feel of them
As they wriggle like landed fish.
When he pulls and tugs and grapples
You'll gasp and gurgle and wish

That you'd never pulled tongues at teacher
Or a stranger behind their back,
As he twists out your tongue and pops it
Into his bobbling, twisted-tongue sack.

ROGER MCGOUGH

Goodfellow

What a rogue! That day his crime
left the police gasping – his light fingers
had taken their breath away

and his victims: a queue
of respectable businessmen standing at a bus-stop
on a wet Monday morning – suddenly

shivering, shocked to see him running away
with their trousers:
he had stolen their dignity.

I saw it! I tried to shout: stop thief!
I couldn't:
he had stolen the words from my mouth

DAVE CALDER

The Kleptomaniac

Beware the Kleptomaniac
Who knows not wrong from right
He'll wait until you turn your back
Then steal everything in sight.

The nose from a snowman
(Be it carrot or coal)

The stick from a blindman
From the beggar his bowl

The smoke from a chimney
The leaves from a tree

A kitten's miaow
(Pretty mean you'll agree)

He'll pinch a used teabag
From out of the pot

A field of potatoes
And scoff the whole lot

(Is baby still there
Asleep in its cot?)

He'll rob the baton
From a conductor on stage

All the books from the library
Page by page

He'll snaffle your shadow
As you bask in the sun

Pilfer the currants
From out of your bun

He'll lift the wind
Right out of your sails

Hold your hand
And make off with your nails

When he's around
Things just disappear

F nnily eno gh I th nk
Th re's one ar und h re!

ROGER McGOUGH

Troll

I'm a troll, foldy roll,
and I'm standing on my bridge.
I'm a troll, foldy roll,
and there's nothing in my fridge.
And I'm getting very hungry
for a nice sam-widge.
So I'll slap you on a slice
and I'll bite – SQUELCH! SQUIDGE!

Or I'll roll you and I'll fold you
in a big foldy roll.
Then I'll lick you and I'll stick you
in my great cake-hole.

I'm a troll, foldy roll,
and I aren't half strong.
And I'm big and I'm hairy
and I don't half pong.
And I gobble up people
though it's nasty and it's wrong.
Now it's time to give a roll
on my noisy dinner GONG!

TONY MITTON

The Sleepy Giant

My age is three hundred and seventy-two.
And I think, with the deepest regret,
How I used to pick up and voraciously chew
The dear little boys whom I met.
I've eaten them raw, in their holiday suits;
I've eaten them curried with rice;
I've eaten them baked, in their jackets and boots.
And found them exceedingly nice.

But now that my jaws are too weak for such fare,
I think it exceedingly rude
To do such a thing, when I'm quite well aware
Little boys do not like to be chewed.

And so I contentedly live upon eels,
And try to do nothing amiss,
And I pass all the time I can spare from my meals
In innocent slumber – like this.

CHARLES E. CARRYL

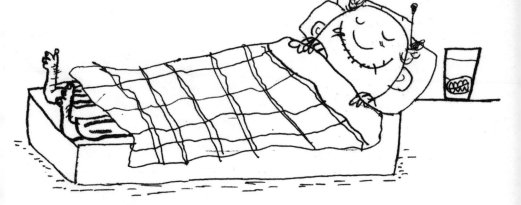

The Story of Little
Suck-a-Thumb

One day, Mamma said: 'Conrad dear.
I must go out and leave you here.
But mind now, Conrad, what I say,
Don't suck your thumb while I'm away.
The great tall tailor always comes
To little boys that suck their thumbs,
And ere they dream what he's about,
He takes his great sharp scissors out
And cuts their thumbs clean off, – and then,
You know, they never grow again.'

Mamma had scarcely turn'd her back,
The thumb was in, Alack! Alack!

The door flew open, in he ran,
The great, long, red-legg'd scissor-man.
Oh! children, see! the tailor's come
And caught out little Suck-a-Thumb.
Snip! Snap! Snip! the scissors go;
And Conrad cries out – Oh! Oh! Oh!
Snip! Snap! Snip! They go so fast,
That both his thumbs are off at last.

SNIP

H. SEYMOUR CUTLERY CO.
PATENT.

SNAP
SNIP!

Mamma comes home; there Conrad stands.
And looks quite sad, and shows his hands, –
'Ah!' said Mamma 'I knew he'd come
To naughty little Suck-a-Thumb.'

DR HOFFMANN

The Devil

From his brimstone bed at the break of day
A walking the Devil is gone
To visit his snug little farm, the earth
And see how his stock goes on.

Over the hill and over the dale,
And he went over the plain,
And backward and forward he switched his long tail
As a gentleman switches his cane.

And how then was the Devil dressed?
Oh! he was in his Sunday's best:
His jacket was red and his breeches were blue
And there was a hole where the tail came through.

SAMUEL TAYLOR COLERIDGE

The Fairies

Up the airy mountain,
    Down the rushy glen,
We daren't go a-hunting
    For fear of little men;
Wee folk, good folk,
    Trooping all together;
Green jacket, red cap,
    And white owl's feather.

Down along the rocky shore
    Some make their home,
They live on crispy pancakes
    Of yellow tide-foam;
Some in the reeds
    Of the black mountain lake,
With frogs for their watch-dogs,
    All night awake.

High on the hill-top
    The old King sits;
He is now so old and gray
    He's nigh lost his wits.
With a bridge of white mist
    Columbkill he crosses,
On his stately journeys
    From Slieveleague to Rosses;

Or going up with music
    On cold starry nights,
To sup with the Queen
    Of the gay Northern Lights.

They stole little Bridget
    For seven years long;
When she came down again
    Her friends were all gone.
They took her lightly back,
    Between the night and morrow,

They thought that she was fast asleep,
    But she was dead with sorrow.
They have kept her ever since
    Deep within the lake,
On a bed of flag-leaves,
    Watching till she wake.

By the craggy hill-side,
    Through the mosses bare,
They have planted thorn-trees
    For pleasure here and there.
Is any man so daring
    As dig them up in spite,
He shall find their sharpest thorns
    In his bed at night.

Up the airy mountain,
 Down the rushy glen,
We daren't go a-hunting
 For fear of little men;
Wee folk, good folk,
 Trooping all together;
Green jacket, red cap,
 And white owl's feather!

WILLIAM ALLINGHAM

The Visitor

A crumbling churchyard, the sea and the moon;
The waves had gouged out grave and bone;
A man was walking, late and alone . . .

He saw a skeleton on the ground;
A ring on a bony hand he found.

He ran home to his wife and gave her the ring.
'Oh, where did you get it?' He said not a thing.

'It's the prettiest ring in the world,' she said,
As it glowed on her finger. They skipped off to bed.

At midnight they woke. In the dark outside,
'Give me my ring!' a chill voice cried.

'What was that, William? What did it say?'
'Don't worry, my dear. It'll soon go away.'

'I'm coming!' A skeleton opened the door.
'Give me my ring!' It was crossing the floor.

'What was that, William? What did it say?'
'Don't worry, my dear. It'll soon go away.'

'I'm touching you now! I'm climbing the bed.'
The wife pulled the sheet right over her head.

It was torn from her grasp and tossed in the air:
'I'll drag you out of your bed by the hair!'

'What was that, William? What did it say?'
'Throw the ring through the window! THROW IT AWAY!'

She threw it. The skeleton leapt from the sill,
Scooped up the ring and clattered downhill,
Fainter . . . and fainter . . . Then all was still.

IAN SERRAILLIER

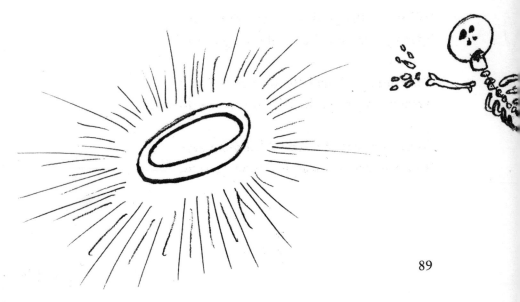

The Huntsman

Kagwa hunted the lion,
   Through bush and forest went his spear.
One day he found the skull of a man
   And said to it, 'How did you come here?'
The skull opened its mouth and said,
   'Talking brought me here.'

Kagwa hurried home;
   Went to the king's chair and spoke:
'In the forest I found a talking skull.'
   The king was silent. Then he said slowly,
'Never since I was born of my mother
   Have I seen or heard of a skull which spoke.'

The king called out to his guards:
   'Two of you now go with him
And find this talking skull;
   But if his tale is a lie
And the skull speaks no word,
   This Kagwa himself must die.'

They rode into the forest;
   For days and nights they found nothing.
At last they saw the skull; Kagwa
   Said to it, 'How did you come here?'
The skull said nothing. Kagwa implored,
   But the skull said nothing.

The guards said, 'Kneel down.'
  They killed him with sword and spear.
Then the skull opened its mouth;
  'Huntsman, how did you come here?'
And the dead man answered,
  'Talking brought me here.'

EDWARD LOWBURY

The Girl Who Lit
the First Fire

In the beginning she thought
she had been chosen to be punished.
And wondering what she might have done
to bring this on herself, she would start
her absentminded whittling and chipping . . .

The pain was terrible.
Who could not try to touch
this beautiful flower, raising it to smell
the strange acrid musk? Look at her hands:
three fingers gone. Thick, pink scars.

Clothes, hair, it all got burnt.
Even neighbours sitting too close
leapt scorched and howling into the bushes.
Shoulders slumped, she would shrug apologies
as they crashed about in the dark.

No one talked about it directly.
No one knew the word for fire.
There was no back-slapping and thanking
the gods for this thing that brought light and heat.
There were only small silences

that seemed to grow
whenever she was around.
But after the accident with her uncle's hut
things changed. Shuffling their feet in the drifts of ash,
the whole village gathered. Asked her kindly to leave.

So there she is. Living up in the mountain.
At night, just able to see her tiny, flickering light,
the villagers huddle in a circle,
pretending not to feel
something is missing.

MANDY COE

Anne Boleyn

A Legend of the Tower of London

Her little feet in scarlet shoon
   They made a pleasant sound
Across the pavement where the moon
   Drew patterns on the ground.

Her clenchèd fists so small and white
   Went beating on the door,
The oaken door that to her sight
   Would open, never more.

She knelt upon the grey cold stone,
   And bowed her head in tears;
She wept, because her heart had grown
   Too wild to hide its fears.

'O Harry love, O dear my King
   I prithee let me in;
Thou couldst not do this cruel thing
   To merry Anne Boleyn.'

She fluttered like some wounded lark
   And ever called his name;
They chained her wrists and through the dark
   They led her to her shame.

So young was she to die alone,
    So fair, and full of tears,
So warm to rest beneath a stone
    Through countless weary years,

That sometimes now men hear her feet
    Across the tower floor,
Her voice beseech, her small hands beat
    Upon that silent door.

'O Harry love, O dear my King
    I prithee let me in;
Thou couldst not do this cruel thing
    To merry Anne Boleyn.'

BARBARA BINGLEY

Lord Lovelace

Lord Lovelace rode home from the wars,
His wounds were black as ice,
While overhead the winter sun
Hung out its pale device.

The lance was tattered in his hand,
Sundered his axe and blade,
And in a bloody coat of war
Lord Lovelace was arrayed.

And he was sick and he was sore
But never sad was he,
And whistled bright as any bird
Upon an April tree.

'Soon, soon,' he cried, 'at Lovelace Hall
Fair Ellen I shall greet,
And she with loving heart and hand
Will make my sharp wounds sweet.

'And Young Jehan the serving-man
Will bring the wine and bread,
And with a yellow link will light
Us to the bridal bed.'

But when he got to Lovelace Hall
Burned were both wall and stack,
And in the stinking moat the tower
Had tumbled on its back.

And none welcomed Lord Lovelace home
Within his castle shell,
And ravaged was the land about
That Lord Lovelace knew well.

Long in his stirrups Lovelace stood
Before his broken door,
And slowly rode he down the hill,
Back to the bitter war.

Nor mercy showed he from that day,
Nor tear fell from his eye,
And rich and poor both fearful were
When Black Lovelace rode by.

This tale is true that now I tell
To woman and to man,
As Fair Ellen is my wife's name
And mine is Young Jehan.

CHARLES CAUSLEY

Empty House

I hate our house when there's no one in
I miss my family and I miss the din.
The rooms and the hallway seem cold and bare
And the silence hangs like dust in the air.
What's that sound upstairs that makes me start
Driving Fear like an icicle through my heart?
I'm imagining things, there's nobody there –
But I have to make sure so I creep up the stair.
I stand holding my breath by the bedroom door
And hear something rustling across the floor.
Then a scratching sound, a tiny cry!
I can't seem to breathe, my throat is dry.
In the silence I hear my own heart beating
And the rumble of water in the central heating.
I should go in but I just don't dare
So I call aloud, 'Is anyone there?'
Nobody answers. I push open the door
A fluttering shadow crosses the floor.
And now I see him, now understand
And I gather him gently in my hands.
'I won't hurt you, my friend. Don't flutter, don't start.'
But his body beats wild like a feathered heart.
Out through the window, watch him wheel and fly
Carrying my fear across the sky.

GARETH OWEN

The Third Fiddler's Story

Old King Cole was a merry old soul,
And a merry old soul was he!
And he called for his wife,
And he called for his pipe,
And he called for his fiddlers three.

When they say merry they mean drunk. A king?
I don't think so, though he could bang the table
like any despot. 'Wife!' he'd say, 'Tell those kids
to get in here and do their violin practice!'
He conducted, the pipe still smoking in his hand.
'Tone deaf, the lot of you. I don't know why I bother.'
When he left the room we played air guitar,
skidding on our knees, heads back
miming huge, tongue-wagging screams.

SIÂN HUGHES

Stepmother

Life with her is a fairytale
She's not like any other
Totally ace and magically cool
My wicked stepmother.

PAUL COOKSON

While I Practise My Piano

I'm being haunted by child spirits.
The door keeps opening.
Will you sit in the room with me
while I practise my piano?
You can even sing –
they won't like that,
your voice would send a bee
careering into a wall,
or would start a cat wailing.
There's the door again,
why are you so slow
at getting in here?
I've got to keep playing –
else the child spirits
will take over my piano
and play tunes of their own,
tunes that might scare me,
and once they got going
they'd never stop, so
please keep me company,
please sit in the room with me
while I practise my piano.

MATTHEW SWEENEY

If

If only my head wasn't heavy as lead
And that glow didn't come from this floor,
If I wasn't so nervy, my mind topsy-turvy,
And there wasn't a shadow on the door,
If my ears didn't hear and my eyes didn't stare at
Things no one else hears or sees,
If the dogs didn't bark, if outside wasn't dark
And I didn't have the shakes in my knees,
If I wasn't so sure that that ear-splitting snore
Couldn't have come from anyone who's alive,
If my heart didn't leap, if my 'flesh' didn't creep
And I was certain this night I'd survive,
If this night weren't so long, if that low mournful song
Didn't freeze every thought in my brain,
If I could be assured that the scuttling I heard
Was only the rats in the drain,
If that shape that I see was the branch of a tree
A shadow cast by the cloud-shrouded moon,
If I could understand why it looks like a hand
Conducting some unearthly tune,
If all that I've said were just in my head
And the whole thing weren't so daunting,
I could return to my grave, feeling ever so brave,
And quite satisfied with my first haunting.

VALERIE BLOOM

The Sad Story of
Terrible Trevor

Terrible Trevor Alucard
Reckoned himself, he said, 'Well Hard.'
His favourite time was after dark.
He stalked the streets, he prowled the park.
'Where are you going?' his mum would shout
And Trev would always answer 'Out!'
At first, it seemed to him enough
To do the usual scary stuff,
Just walk about in studs and leather,
Chains and buckles and whatever
But soon he found this rather boring
Like playing football without scoring.
'What can I do tomorrow night
To give everyone a proper fright?'
He asked himself, then scratched his head.
'The trouble with this town – it's dead!'
To tell the truth you'd seldom find
A fresh thought crossing Trevor's mind,

But suddenly he cried out 'Hey,
The churchyard's got a right of way
Past all those crosses, angels' wings
And stones and spooky graves and things.
It's just the place to hang around,
To tiptoe up without a sound
And then with a blood-curdling cry
To leap out on any passers-by.'
So next day he spent his pocket-money
(All of it, every single penny)
On a cloak and fangs – vampire attire –
From *Van Helsing's Costume Hire*
And took it home. 'What's that you've got?'
Asked Trevor's mum. 'I'll tell you what,
Mind your own business, woman!' Sad,
But Trev gave answers like his dad
And just like Dad he snarled and swore
Then stomped upstairs and slammed the door.

So night arrived, and fit to burst,
Trev was ready to do his worst.
I tell you, he could hardly wait
To dress up at the churchyard gate.
Once there he donned his vampire kit,
Just as he'd hoped, a perfect fit.
Now for a passer-by to scare.
As if the answer to a prayer
And much to Trevor's cruel delight
A hurrying figure came in sight.
At first it seemed to be the vicar
Except he was moving rather quicker,
Sort of floating down the path
With a sort of rather nasty laugh
(Crepuscular and melancholy)
Which Trev could tell was far from holy,
And then, alas, – Oh send us grace! –
The two of them met face to face
Like shadows looking in a mirror,
One with a grin, the other terror.

This was now way beyond a joke.
The grin flashed pointed fangs then spoke:
'My, what a silly boy you are,
Pretending to be Dracula
When anyone can see that you
Really haven't got a clue
About blood suction and all that.
You couldn't scare a witch's cat!
Your cloak's too short, your fangs are fake,
Your whole equipment's a mistake,
You should be drinking Seven-Up
Or bedtime cocoa from a cup
Instead of scaring little kids
With talk of garlic, coffin lids
And all the necks you're going to bite.
Still, Trev, since we've met tonight
We might as well become acquainted
(By this time Trev had nearly fainted!)
So shut your eyes and count to ten.
You won't have to pretend again.

Our meeting here is most fortuitous.
I need an apprentice, Trev, and you it is!
You've an awful lot to learn, I know,
But you're keen enough, it seems. Let's go,
Tomorrow is another day
And Transylvania's quite a way!'

With that, a flash and a clap of thunder
A cloak was swirled and Trev tucked under.
He might have given a muffled shout
But there was nobody else about
Except the cold dead, long engraved,
Indifferent to how a boy behaved
And, anyway, far too deep to hear
Or, if they did, too late to care.
Now, in the churchyard, one more stone
Under the yew tree all alone
Says Trevor Alucard RIP
Except he *doesn't*, believe you me!

JOHN MOLE

Leviathan

Something has grown too big for the pond:
first the moorhens disappeared
then the ducks (corner-of-the-eye stuff,
nothing strictly attributable).
The Canada geese stayed, but looked as if they knew
something they'd rather not think about.

A goat on the village green went mad overnight.
Then pensioners living nearby
started to peg out: heart attacks mostly
and always at Meals-on-Wheels time
(the body on the rug, the cartons emptied).
Alice Weevil went missing altogether.

A builder up a ladder, on his mobile,
didn't at first hear the flub of something
working its way up the rungs behind him.
'Quick, Reg,' were his last words –
'get the pond drained – don't wait
for the Council – there's a huge, unbelievable –'

CONNIE BENSLEY

Limps

Limps lie around
occasionally in pairs
in wait for someone walking
completely unawares

At the sound of a footstep
they prick up their ears
licking their lips
as the victim appears

They whiplash the foot
as it passes by
then sink their teeth
as you let out a cry

Holding fast to your ankle
they feed off the pain
as you stumble like someone
dragging a chain

And when the doctor declares
'It's only a sprain'
they've scuttled off cackling
to lie in wait again

ROGER McGOUGH

The Boyhood of Dracula

So we let him join us
In the game of Hide and Seek
Because Joanna said we ought,
She being the biggest of us all
And bossy with it.
And him standing there
All hunched and trembling
In the thin snow by the stable door
Watching us like some poor lost soul
With those great eyes he had.
Well, you'd be a thing of stone
To take no pity on the boy.
You never saw a soul
So pale and woebegone;
His pinched nose raw with cold
And naught to keep the bitter wind
The right side of his bones
But that old bit of musty cloak
He always seems to wear.

Poor little mite
You'd think, to watch,
He'd never played the game before.
Maureen Cantelow,
The parson's youngest girl
From Norton Campion way,

She found him straight away
Hardly bothering to hide at all
Among the meal sacks
In the lower barn.
Poor girl,
She must have cut herself
In there somehow
For as I spied them
Running hand in hand below
She sowed fresh seeds of crimson blood
Across ridged and bitter snow.

GARETH OWEN

Vlad

Vlad   ve
vampire vlies
vrough   voonlight
velvet vat vings vlitter-
vlutter. Vlad's very vain vith
vangs vo vlong very vite
vrough vlesh vlike vutter.
Vlad vears a vast vile
violet vest villed vith
vermin vrom ve vault
vich vongs vorse van
virty vultures — vo
vonder victims
vaint   vand
vall! Vicious,
vulgar, vlood-
vrinking, vad,
v i o l e n t ,
villainous —
vot a vlad

DAVE CALDER

112

Wicked

I'm wicked, such a wicked person,
In all the world there's not a worse 'un.
My wickedness is so primeval
I swear I'm absolutely evil
And so unutterably horrid
Two horns have sprouted from my forehead.
I clop around on devil feet.
With devil forks I spear my meat,
Then tear it in my devil jaws.
My nails are black and curved like claws.
My teeth are jaggy like a shark.
I jump on people in the dark.
I roll my devil eyes about,
And, with my wicked devil shout,
Yell dreadful, doomy, devil things.
I've got these pterodactyl wings,
And poisonous snakes instead of hair
(You might not see them, but they're there),
I'm wicked and I just don't care.

JOHN WHITWORTH

113

Wicked or What

The flying beetle that buzzed my hairdo.
The crow that messed next door's Mondeo.
The sheepdog that licked my tongue
(won't leave it hanging out like that again).
Wicked. One way or the other. Wicked.

My baby sister who put the art into fart.
My cousin Harry's puce denim shirt.
The way the weather winds Aunty up.
Dad's word when he got caught in his zip.
Wicked. One way or the other. Wicked.

The jeans that make me look fit.
Chocolate in my pocket when it's hot.
The skateboard that put me in traction.
My face caught out (by me) in a reflection.
Wicked. One way or the other. Wicked.

JO SHAPCOTT

Eve

If I'd *known* Eve,
I'd have told her
Of that fast
Descending boulder.
But as she was
Just a stranger,
It seemed wrong
To mention danger.

COLIN WEST

Claud

Claud cut himself up with a knife
To please his little nieces.
He lived a most unhappy life,
But now he'll rest in pieces.

COLIN WEST

Mafia Cats

We're the Mafia cats
 Bugsy, Franco annd Toni
We're crazy for pizza
 With hot pepperoni

We run all the rackets
 From gambling to vice
On St Valentine's Day
 We massacre mice

We always wear shades
 To show that we're meanies
Big hats and sharp suits
 And drive Lamborghinis

We're the Mafia cats
 Bugsy, Franco and Toni
Love Sicilian wine
 And cheese macaraoni

But we have a secret
 (And if you dare tell
You'll end up with the kitten
 At the bottom of the well

Or covered in concrete
  And thrown into the deep
For this is one secret
  you really must keep).

We're the Cosa Nostra
  Run the scams and the fiddles
But at home we are
  Mopsy, Ginger and Tiddles.

ROGER MCGOUGH

Macavity: The Mystery Cat

Macavity's a Mystery Cat: he's called the Hidden Paw —
For he's the master criminal who can defy the Law.
He's the bafflement of Scotland Yard, the Flying Squad's despair:
For when they reach the scene of crime — *Macavity's not there!*

Macavity, Macavity, there's no one like Macavity,
He's broken every human law, he breaks the law of gravity.
His powers of levitation would make a fakir stare,
And when you reach the scene of crime — *Macavity's not there!*
You may seek him in the basement, you may look up in the air —
But I tell you once and once again, *Macavity's not there!*

Macavity's a ginger cat, he's very tall and thin;
You would know him if you saw him, for his eyes are sunken in.
His brow is deeply lined with thought, his head is highly domed;
His coat is dusty from neglect, his whiskers are uncombed.
He sways his head from side to side, with movements like a snake;
And when you think he's half asleep, he's always wide awake.

Macavity, Macavity, there's no one like Macavity,
For he's a fiend in feline shape, a monster of depravity.
You may meet him in a by-street, you may see him in the square —
But when a crime's discovered, then *Macavity's not there!*

He's outwardly respectable. (They say he cheats at cards.)
And his footprints are not found in any file of Scotland Yard's.
And when the larder's looted, or the jewel-case is rifled,
Or when the milk is missing, or another Peke's been stifled,
Or the greenhouse glass is broken, and the trellis past repair —
Ay, there's the wonder of the thing! *Macavity's not there!*

And when the Foreign Office find a Treaty's gone astray,
Or the Admiralty lose some plans and drawings by the way,
There may be a scrap of paper in the hall or on the stair —
But it's useless to investigate — *Macavity's not there!*
And when the loss has been disclosed, the Secret Service say:
'It must have been Macavity!' — but he's a mile away.
You'll be sure to find him resting, or a-licking of his thumbs,
Or engaged in doing complicated long division sums.

Macavity, Macavity, there's no one like Macavity,
There never was a Cat of such deceitfulness and suavity.
He always has an alibi, and one or two to spare:
At whatever time the deed took place
                    — MACAVITY WASN'T THERE!
And they say that all the Cats whose wicked deeds are widely known
(I might mention Mungojerrie, I might mention Griddlebone)
Are nothing more than agents for the Cat who all the time
Just controls their operations: the Napoleon of Crime!

T.S. ELIOT

A Ransom for a Cat

Wicked Kings and kidnaps
were some kids' sort of dream
    . . . having cruel step-mums
    evil awful queens . . .
They read up all these stories
they read for hours and hours
    witches in the wild woods
    princesses stuck in towers
But I was into action
and ransoms were my thing
So I captured next door's tabbie
(with a fishcake on a string)

    I hid him in my wardrobe
    with my new school coat
    and wrote in ransom writing
    a little ransom note

I waited and I waited
the cat went crazy mad
it piddled in the cupboard
and it piddled on my bag . . .
It tore the bedroom curtains
it bit me on the knee
it did things in the corner
and it had massive flea!

The answer came next morning
in writing bold and black . . .
Thanks for taking Stinky
please never send him back.

PETER DIXON

Song of the Worms

We have been underground too long,
we have done our work,
we are many and one,
we remember when we were human.

We have lived among roots and stones,
we have sung but no one has listened,
we come into the open air
at night only to love

which disgusts the soles of boots,
their leather strict religion.
We know what a boot looks like
when seen from underneath,
we know the philosophy of boots,
their metaphysic of kicks and ladders.
We are afraid of boots
but contemptuous of the foot that needs them.

Soon we will invade like weeds,
everywhere but slowly;
the captive plants will rebel
with us, fences will topple,
brick walls ripple and fall,

there will be no more boots.
Meanwhile we eat dirt
and sleep; we are waiting
under your feet.
When we say Attack
you will hear nothing
at first.

MARGARET ATWOOD

The Snake's Revenge

You could never imagine me,
not in a zillion years,
I'm far beyond the scope of
your wildest nightmares or fears.

But I'm here, at the edge of your universe,
a creature of immeasurable girth.
Hatred has made me huge, and now
I'm the snake that will swallow the earth.

And I'm moving ever closer,
I've already gobbled up stars,
I've unhinged my jaws and soon I'll be ready
to take a crack at Mars.

And when I finally reach you
I'll tell you now what I'll do
I shall wrap my coils round your planet
and squeeze the breath out of you.

And this will be my revenge
from the time that I was cursed,
for eternity spent on my belly,
for the dust that I ate, for my thirst.

And remember well, if you will,
for a snake is nobody's friend,
I was there at the very beginning
and I'll be there at the end.

For the world won't finish in flame
or by drowning in a flood.
It won't be wholly engulfed
in an ocean of angry mud.

There'll be no explosion, no fracture,
no tremors from a last earthquake.
I tell you now, this world will end
in the belly of a snake.

BRIAN MOSES

My Pony

I had a little pony,
I called him Dapple Grey;
I lent him to a lady
To ride a mile away.

She whipped him, she lashed him,
She drove him through the mire.
I would not lend my pony now
For all the lady's hire.

ANON

Lone Dog

I'm a lean dog, a keen dog, a wild dog and lone,
I'm a rough dog, a tough dog, hunting on my own!
I'm a bad dog, a mad dog, teasing silly sheep;
I love to sit and bay the moon and keep fat souls from sleep.

I'll never be a lap dog, licking dirty feet,
A sleek dog, a meek dog, cringing for my meat.
Not for me the fireside, the well-filled plate;
But shut door and sharp stone and cuff and kick and hate.

Not for me the other dogs, running by my side,
Some have run a short while, but none of them would bide.
O mine is still the lone trail, the hard trail, the best
Wide wind and wild stars and the hunger of the quest.

IRENE MCLEOD

Elegy on the Death of a Mad Dog

Good people all, of every sort,
    Give ear unto my song;
And if you find it wondrous short,
    It cannot hold you long.

In Islington there was a man,
    Of whom the world might say,
That still a godly race he ran,
    Whene'er he went to pray.

A kind and gentle heart he had,
    To comfort friends and foes;
The naked every day he clad,
    When he put on his clothes.

And in that town a dog was found,
    As many dogs there be,
Both mongrel, puppy, whelp and hound,
    And curs of low degree.

This dog and man at first were friends;
    But when a pique began,
The dog, to gain some private ends,
    Went mad and bit the man.

Around from all the neighbouring streets
  The wondering neighbours ran,
And swore the dog had lost his wits,
  To bite so good a man.

The wound it seem'd both sore and sad
  To every Christian eye;
And while they swore the dog was mad,
  They swore the man would die.

But soon a wonder came to light,
  That show'd the rogues they lied:
The man recover'd of the bite,
  The dog it was that died.

OLIVER GOLDSMITH

Max

(likes to be with people
but people don't like to be with Max)

Max is a dog with a problem
the sort of problem it's a job to ignore
the first time they all thought it was funny
but not any more
picture the scene this home loving hound
is sleeping by the fire with the family round
he wakes up and makes a little sound
little Albert gets it first
he's nearest to the ground
Albert's Mum gets wind of it
and she says open the door
and whatever we've been feeding him
I don't think we should give him no more
Max does another one like old kippers
wakes up Daddy in his fireside slippers
Daddy wakes up and says open the door
Albert says it's open Dad I did it when he did it before
then Mum says it's hard to relax with Max about
yesterday it happened while we were out in the car
and it's a small car
and Granny she was sick
she's not used to it like we are

maybe we should swap him for a budgerigar
Max is smelly
he can spoil your telly
but luckily
he's not an elephant

J OHN H EGLEY

The Elephant

Elephant, who brings death.
Elephant, a spirit in the bush.
With a single hand
He can pull two palm trees to the ground.
If he had two hands
He would tear the sky like an old rag.
The spirit who eats dog,
The spirit who eats ram,
The spirit who eats
A whole palm fruit with its thorns.
With his four mortal legs
He tramples down the grass.
Wherever he walks
The grass is forbidden to stand up again.

YORUBA PEOPLE, AFRICA

Dragon at a Party

Sidles in slowly and slyly and seedily.
Wanders round wilily, wheedling wheezily
Grinning and greeting all gratingly greasily,
Chummily, cheerily chattering cheesily.

Leerily, beerily back-biting easily.
Simpering simply salaciously sleazily.
Pedalling scandal unpleasantly pleasedly.
Eavesdropping evilly, eyes popping beadily.

Hears his hosts' infant is in bed, diseasedly.
Creeps upstairs sneakily, creakily, weaselly.
Finds where the poor mite is quarantined queasily.
Quiets their darling, his teeth closing tweezerly.

Blood flesh and bone are all cleared away speedily,
Lovingly licked up and guzzled down greedily.
Dragons don't mind their meat sickly or measly.

'Wonderful party!' he tells them all breezily,
Slips through the door and leaves, easy-peasily.

NICK TOCZEK

Shadow

Across my bedroom wall
Flapping its giant grey wings:
a monster.

Across my bedroom lamp
fluttering its small brown wings:
a moth.

MICHAEL ROSEN

The Spiders Cast Their Spell

Break our
web
Break our
universe

        We in return
        will bless
        you with a curse

May your two legs
grow to be eight

        May your sleep be
        too light
        for the weight
        of your dreams

May your house
collapse
at the slight
touch of a breeze

        And as you sit
        among the ruin
        of your memories

May you wish
for thread to spin
May you wish
for thread to spin.

JOHN AGARD

The Hump

The Camel's hump is an ugly lump
   Which well you may see at the Zoo;
But uglier yet is the hump we get
   From having too little to do.

Kiddies and grown-ups too-oo-oo,
If we haven't enough to do-oo-oo,
     We get the hump—
     Cameelious hump—
The hump that is black and blue!

We climb out of bed with a frouzly head,
   And a snarly-yarly voice.
We shiver and scowl and we grunt and we growl
   At our bath and our boots and our toys;

And there ought to be a corner for me
(And I know there is one for you)
     When we get the hump—
     Cameelious hump—
The hump that is black and blue!

The cure for this ill is not to sit still,
   Or frowst with a book by the fire;
But to take a large hoe and a shovel also,
   And dig till you gently perspire;

And then you will find that the sun and the
    wind,
And the Djinn of the Garden too,
    Have lifted the hump—
    The horrible hump—
The hump that is black and blue!

I get it as well as you-oo-oo—
If I haven't enough to do-oo-oo!
    We all get hump—
    Cameelious hump—
Kiddies and grown-ups too!

RUDYARD KIPLING

The Greedy Alligator

I have a rather greedy pet,
A little alligator;
When he my younger sister met,
He opened wide and ate her.

But soon he learned that he was wrong
To eat the child in question,
For he felt bad before too long,
And suffered indigestion.

This story seems to prove to me
That he who rudely gobbles
Will soon regret his gluttony
And get the collywobbles.

COLIN WEST

How Doth the Little Crocodile

How doth the little crocodile
   Improve his shining tail;
And pour the waters of the Nile
   On every golden scale!

How cheerfully he seems to grin,
   How neatly spreads his claws,
And welcomes little fishes in,
   With gently smiling jaws!

LEWIS CARROLL

The Art of Dying

We were nine years old when we killed Brendan.
An enemy sniper, shot
with a sawn-off broomstick,
he died without question.

And unlike other lads,
always arguing for their lives,
Brendan would lie
draped like a sandbag over the wall,
his weapon fallen from his hand.

You could even poke him with a foot,
roll him over and thumb up the lid
of one flickering eye.

We took his death for granted
— most shots going wild
— knowing we could always save
the last bullet for Brendan.

Then one day I saw him
walking past our front hedge.
You're dead! I shouted,
not even bothering to aim.

But Brendan carried on by,
followed by his dad; a towering bloke,
who scowled at me and pointed
one meaty finger.

I didn't think twice.
And with my cheek pressed down
into the sharp, damp grass, I felt
the safety of being dead.

MANDY COE

Legend

The rooms were mirrors
for that luminous face,
the morning windows ferned
with cold. Outside
a level world of snow.

Voiceless birds in the trees
like notes in the books
in the piano stool.
She let us suck top-of-the-milk
burst from the bottles like corks.

Then wrapped shapeless
we stumped to the park
between the parapets of snow
in the wake of the shovellers,
cardboard rammed in the tines of garden forks.

The lake was an empty rink
and I stepped out,
pushing my sister first
onto its creaking floor.
When I brought her home,

shivering, wailing, soaked,
they thought me a hero.
But I still wake at night
to hear the Snow Queen's knuckles crack,
black water running fingers through the ice.

GILLIAN CLARKE

Power

No one we knew had ever stopped a train.
Hardly daring to breathe, I waited
Belly-down with my brother
In a dry ditch.
Watching through the green thickness
Of grass and willows.
Stuffed with crumpled newspapers,
The shirt and pants looked real enough
Stretched out across the rails. I felt my heart
Beating against the cool ground,
And the terrible long screech of the train's
Braking began. We had done it.

Then it was in front of us—
A hundred iron wheels, tearing like time
Into a red flannel and denim, shredding the child
We had made—until it finally stopped.
My brother jabbed at me,
Pointed down the tracks. A man
Had climbed out of the engine, was running
In our direction, waving his arms,
Screaming that he would kill us—
Whoever we were.
Then, very close to the spot
Where we hid, he stomped and cursed
As the rags and papers scattered
Over the gravel from our joke.

I tried to remember which of us
That red shirt had belonged to,
But morning seemed too long ago, and the man
Was falling, sobbing, to his knees.
I couldn't stop watching.
My brother lay next to me,
His hands covering his ears,
His face pressed tight to the ground.

CORRINE HALES

This is a Photograph of Me

It was taken some time ago.
At first it seems to be
a smeared
print: blurred lines and grey flecks
blended with the paper;

then, as you scan
it, you see in the left-hand corner
a thing that is like a branch: part of a tree
(balsam or spruce) emerging
and, to the right, halfway up
what ought to be a gentle
slope, a small frame house.

In the background there is a lake,
and beyond that, some low hills.

(The photograph was taken
the day after I drowned.

I am in the lake, in the centre
of the picture, just under the surface.

It is difficult to say where
precisely, or to say
how large or small I am:

the effect of water
on light is a distortion

but if you look long enough,
eventually
you will be able to see me.)

MARGARET ATWOOD

Wicked

Got no horns or twirly tail.
Got no leer or banshee wail.
But I'm wicked. Yeah, wicked.

Got no shiny, bright-red skin.
Got no cloak as black as sin.
But I'm wicked. Yeah, wicked.

Got no wand with fizz-&-spark.
Got no spellbook deep-&-dark.
But I'm wicked. Yeah, wicked.

Don't come rising from the swamp.
Don't go, '*Grunt and groan,*' and stomp.
Don't come bubbling from the mud.
Don't grind bones, no, don't drink blood.
Don't chew human flesh for food.
Ain't no way no gruesome dude.

Ain't no kind of grisly ghoul.
Tell you what, though, kid – **I'm cool!**
So I'm wicked. Yeah, wicked.
Said, wicked. Yeah, wicked.
Oooooh!

TONY MITTON

Iciclist

First, he was put on a tricycle,
when he didn't mind looking a fool.

Later, a racing bicycle
gave him some status at school.

Now he gets about on an icicle –
the ultimate in cool.

CHRISTOPHER REID

This Poem is Soooo *Prop*

Cool used to be
A really cool word,
Then it warmed up slightly
And flew away on old lady's wings.

Then Wicked
Was Wicked
Now it's more ancient than my Uncle Jack,
(That's my ancient Uncle Jack we're talking about).

So now I invent a new word every day
Just to keep one step ahead.

Last week I was
Snail, Wallpaper, Buckle, Hen's teeth,
But they're so last week.

Yesterday I was Crocodile
But that's Yesterday's thing.

Today I'm *prop*,
The *proppest* kid on our street.

Till tomorrow.

IAN MCMILLAN

We Real Cool

The Pool Players.
Seven at the Golden Shovel.

We real cool. We
Left school. We

Lurk late. We
Strike straight. We

Sing sin. We
Thin gin. We

Jazz June. We
Die soon.

GWENDOLYN BROOKS

Bully

The playground bully
   barged up to me.
He blustered. He cursed.
   He threatened big trouble.
And the speech balloon –
   or speech bubble –
that floated above his head
   like his own private moon
grew heavier
   and heavier
with the many vile and violent
   things he said.
It bulged. It sagged.
   It seemed about to burst.
I thought of getting a pin
   and sticking it in
to help it along,
   but one sharp look
was all it took.
   One look was enough.
With a great pop –
   or splat – it shattered,
spattering him
   from head to foot
with all the disgusting stuff
   that had just come out of his mouth.

I tell you,
   that made him stop.
That made him strangely silent.
   That made him sing a new song.

C H R I S T O P H E R R E I D

Something *made* me do it!
(To Declan)

In the very darkest corner of the very darkest room
Something's hiding, something's biding – something small
        and hunkered down.
It's a strategy for mischief, grinning in the gloom.

Lying doggo in your larynx there's a verb waiting its chance.
It's not the verb 'to laugh', 'to sing', or otherwise 'to dance';
It's 'to whip up merry hell' in both the past and future tense.

There's a small voice in your brain-box that is telling you to do
Something sicko, something whacko, something no one else
        would do,
Like sneeze onto the smorgasbord or dump glue in the stew.

There's a cupboard in your bedroom stuffed with swag and
        loot and pelf.
Who put it there – a djinn, perhaps, a hobgoblin, an elf,
Or a kid called Robin Goodfellow, a.k.a. yourself?

There's a twinkle in your eye, my friend, that wasn't there before.
It says, 'Go on, just *do* it; and then do it some more –
Whatever's mad or bad or just a tad outside the law.'

There's someone in the mirror who looks a bit like you
But second glance reveals a creature straight from Satan's zoo
Who ate your maths homework and put the gerbil down the loo.

There's a little green-eyed demon floating just above your head
Who makes you say the kind of things you never would have said
If only you had thought of something worse to say instead.

In the space behind the curtain, in the space behind the door,
In the space behind the fireplace, the space beneath the floor,
Lives whatever makes you do the things your friends get
      punished for.

And somewhere in your deepest dream, a vast and shiny vault
Secured with coded padlocks and a krypton laser-bolt
Holds all the things that happened THAT WERE SIMPLY
      NOT YOUR FAULT!

DAVID HARSENT

The Village Burglar

Under the spreading gooseberry bush
  The village burglar lies;
The burglar is a hairy man
  With whiskers round his eyes.

He goes to church on Sundays;
  He hears the Parson shout;
He puts a penny in the plate
  And takes a shilling out.

ANON

The Smiling Villain

Forth from his den to steal he stole,
His bags of chink he chunk,
And many a wicked smile he smole,
And many a wink he wunk.

ANON

Neighbourhood Watch

It's a sin
It's a crime
Now we can't tell the time
Our neighbourhood watch
Has been stolen!

ROGER MCGOUGH

Barbara the Barbarian

Barbara was a barbarian.
Her mother was a librarian,
Her father was a grammarian
And her brother pretended to be a Rastafarian

But Barbara was a barbarian, and dwelt in Gaul
Which wasn't convenient at all.
Still she made her way to Rome for the Fall
(Despite being only 4ft 11$\frac{1}{2}$ inches tall),

Having first packed her
Shield for when the Centurians attacked her,
A helmet in case anybody hacked her
And her sun-tan lotion (factor

8). It was some shindig, the Fall of Rome,
With a river of bloody foam
Lapping the top of the highest dome
But when Barbara finally went home

And they asked her about the fray
And all the legions she helped to slay
And whether she'd enjoyed it, all she would say
Was, 'Yeah, I suppose . . . Yeah, it was okay.'

SIMON RAE

The Pirate

Oh, the blithery, blathery pirate
(His name, I believe, is Claude),
His manner is sullen and irate,
And his humor is vulgar and broad.

He has often been known to imprison
His friends in the hold dark and dank,
Or lash them up high on the mizzen,
Or force them to stroll down a plank.

He will selfishly ask you to dig up
Some barrels of ill-gotten gold,
And if you so much as just higgup,
He'll leave you to fill up the hole.

He may cast you adrift in a rowboat
(He has no reaction to tears)
Or put you ashore without NO boat
On an island and leave you for years.

He's a rotter, a wretch and a sinner,
He's foul as a fellow can be,
But if you invite him to dinner,
Oh, please sit him next to me!

SHEL SILVERSTEIN

Song of the Galley-slaves

We pulled for you when the wind was against us and the sails were low.
   Will you never let us go?
We ate bread and onions when you took towns, or ran aboard
   quickly when you were beaten back by the foe.
The captains walked up and down the deck in fair weather singing
   songs, but we were below.
We fainted with our chins on the oars and you did not see that they
   were idle, for we still swung to and fro.
   Will you never let us go?
The salt made our oar-handles like shark-skin; our knees were cut to
   the bone with salt-cracks; our hair was stuck to our foreheads; and
   our lips were cut to the gums, and you whipped us because we
   could not row.
   Will you never let us go?
But, in a little time, we shall run out of the port-holes as the water
   runs along the oar-blade, and though you tell the others to row
   after us you will never catch us till you catch the oar-thresh and
   tie up the winds in the belly of the sail. Aho!
   Will you never let us go?

RUDYARD KIPLING

If All the Seas

If all the seas were one sea,
What a great sea that would be!
If all the trees were one tree,
What a great tree that would be!
And if all the axes were one axe,
What a great axe that would be!
And if all the men were one man,
What a great man that would be!
And if the great man took the great axe
And cut down the great tree,
And let it fall into the great sea,
What a splish-splash that would be!

ANON

The World's Worst Super-Villain

I'm a total super-villain, me:
I'm evil to the core;
My problem is I'm well-behaved
And never break the law.

I'd be so good at being bad,
I'd live for violent crime,
If only I could just stop
Being gentle all the time.

I worked hard at all my homework
For the Villains' School Of Vice,
But they failed me for not cheating
And for being far too nice.

I'd build a giant super-bomb
To blast the world apart;
But as I like it as it is,
I haven't got the heart.

I'm the world's worst super-villain.
I just haven't got a clue.
I'm hard-working, kind and honest.
I'm a failure through and through.

DAVID BATEMAN

Confessions of a
Failed Super Villain

1. The ballerina disguise was a mistake.
2. So was the blonde curly wig and the pigtails.
3. Water pistols aren't that scary really when it comes to world domination.
4. I should have taken over the Post Office Tower in London, not the Post Office in Anglesey.
5. I shouldn't have tried to start on Wednesday afternoon when it was half day closing.
6. Thursday morning would have been better if I hadn't overslept and got stuck in a queue behind thirteen pensioners.
7. My demands should have been displayed on the World Wide Net on my SuperVillainDotCom Website . . . and not on Hospital Radio.
8. Threatening to blow up a football and not a football stadium was a costly typing error.
9. Stealing three packets of Smarties from the corner shop perhaps wasn't the most dramatic beiginning to a potential reign of terror.
10. Calling myself the **Wickedly Evil Tyrant** and then signing my initials didn't frighten anybody.

Paul Cookson

Charlotte O'Neil's Song

You rang your bell and I answered.
I polished your parquet floor.
I scraped out your grate
and I washed your plate
and I scrubbed till my hands were raw.

You lay on a silken pillow.
I lay on an attic cot.
That's the way it should be, you said.
That's the poor girl's lot.
You dined at eight
and slept till late.
I emptied your chamber pot.
The rich man earns his castle, you said.
The poor deserve the gate.

But I'll never say 'sir'
or 'thank you ma'am'
and I'll never curtsy more.
You can bake your bread
and make your bed
and answer your own front door.

I've cleaned your plate
and I've cleaned your house
and I've cleaned the clothes you wore.
But now you're on your own, my dear.
I won't be there any more.
And I'll eat when I please
and I'll sleep where I please

and you can open your own front door.

FIONA FARRELL

Portrait of My Lover
as a Teaspoon

What I need, O Lord,
is a pot
to boil my ex-husband in, O Lord,
and reduce the resulting juices
to a concentrate
it will take a good long thousand years
to sweeten –
and then, O Lord,
I hope he can go to Heaven
to be fed to Your little cherubim
by the teaspoonful.

SELIMA HILL

Notting Hill Polka

We've – had –
A Body in the house
   Since Father passed away:
He took bad on
Saturday night an' he
   Went the followin' day:

Mum's – pulled –
The blinds all down
   An' bought some Sherry Wine,
An' we've put the tin
What the Arsenic's in
   At the bottom of the Ser-pen-tine!

W. BRIDGES-ADAMS

167

Vanity Song

What shall I bring you
now that you've gone?
Cutworm, gall-fly and codling moth.

What will I sing now
instead of a song?
The cry of a gull and the curlew's call.

What can I make you
for breaking this bond?
I will make you remember the emptying night,

and the shame will be your reward.

ROBIN ROBERTSON

Buinneach Buí

Let runny as buttermilk
Be the diarrhoea
I curse you to suffer with
For one entire year.

TRADITIONAL IRISH CHARM
Translated by Ian Duhig

Entrails

I am convinced that digestion is the great secret of life.
Rev. Sydney Smith

Twenty two feet of wonders
Twenty two feet of woes:
Why we're obliged to have so many yards of them
Nobody really knows.

Sometimes they lie retentive,
Sometimes they're wild and free,
Sometimes they writhe and get madly expulsive
The moment you're out to tea.

Entrails don't care for travel,
Entrails don't care for stress:
Entrails are better kept folded inside you
For outside, they make a mess.

Entrails put hara-kiri
High on their list of hates:
Also they loathe being spread on the carpet
While someone haruspicates.

Twenty two feet of wonders
Twenty two feet of woes:
Why we're obliged to have so many yards of them
Nobody really knows.

CONNIE BENSLEY

Say Cheese

after Shakespeare's Sonnet No 18

Shall I compare you to a plate of cheese?
You made me crumble, turned my heart to jelly,
Oh I had a case of trembling knees,
For Barry, the big cheese (somewhat smelly)
Just listen bud, don't call me darling, eh?
I'm not totally dim though you melted my heart
I saw you snog Samantha on Sunday,
I'm so cheesed off, it's time for us to part!
Your cheesiness will never fade,
Though I admit you had me in a pickle,
Nor shall you brag that I was betrayed
Barry, so un-mature and fickle
So long as girls have brains to stop and think
They'd say you're a moron and you stink!

ANDREW FUSEK PETERS

He and She

To show her how much he loved her
He bought her a beautiful rose,
But it gave her a fit of the sneezes
So she twisted the end of his nose.

To show her how much he loved her
He bought her some Belgian chocs,
But a caramel pulled out her fillings
So she clobbered his head with the box.

To show her how much he loved her
He bought her a basket of pears,
But the one that she bit had a worm in
So she pinched him and kicked him downstairs.

So he bought her some yogurt and treacle
Which he mixed with cold custard and dirt,
And to show her how much he loved her —
Poured the lot down the front of her shirt.

RICHARD EDWARDS

Midnight Street

in the midnight street
two gangs meet:
they are big men
fists bunched
muscles knotted
big boots on their feet

under the lamp-posts' glare
they stare each other down

no-one speaks a word:
behind them on the wall
the graffiti says it all

nobody spits
nobody curses
but no-one budges

they have come back
still bearing the grudges
they've lived with
since they were boys

then out into the long dark space
between them
somebody rolls a ball

DAVE WARD

173

Poem

I don't like pretty parties
With girls and all that stuff
Playing games and singing
And grub that's made of puff

　I like proper parties
　Where you charge around the place
　Wrestle on the sofas
　– Jump and yell and race

I like a bit of action
Football down the hall
Kung-fu on the carpet
Banging on the wall

　I like some sausage chucking
　Sandwich throwing too
　Pulling at the curtains
　Hiding in the loo.

I like it best in bedrooms
And poking all around
Getting ghetto blasters
And turning up the sound

I love it in the bathrooms
Playing with the showers
Letting go the hamster
And picking garden flowers

Yea! I love a decent party
But they're few and far between
People don't invite me
[If you see what I mean]

So: If your birthday's coming
And you'd like some proper fun
Then please, oh please! Remember
That I'd really love to come.

PETER DIXON

If People Disapprove of You . . .

Make being disapproved of your hobby.
Make being disapproved of your aim.
Devise new ways of scoring points
In the Being Disapproved Of Game.

Let them disapprove in their dozens.
Let them disapprove in their hoards.
You'll find that being disapproved of
Builds character, brings rewards

Just like any form of striving.
Don't be arrogant; don't coast
On your high disapproval rating.
Try to be disapproved of most.

At this point, if it's useful
Draw a pie chart or a graph.
Show it to someone who disapproves.
When they disapprove, just laugh.

Count the emotions you provoke:
Anger, suspicion, shock.
One point for each of these and two
For every boat you rock.

Feel yourself warming to your task –
You do it bloody well.
At last you've found an area
In which you can excel.

Savour the thrill of risk without
The fear of getting caught.
Whether they sulk or scream or pout,
Enjoy your newfound sport.

Meanwhile all those who disapprove
While you are having fun
Won't even know your game exists
So tell yourself you've won.

SOPHIE HANNAH

GBH

'Kick 'is teeth in,' said Grandma,
'Punch 'im 'ard in the eye,
Chuck 'im out of the window,
It's only ten storeys 'igh.'

'But Gran, it's the man from the council,
He's shown you his badge, and I.D.,
You can't go round beating up people
Let's all have a nice cup of tea.'

'I've come,' said the man from the council,
'Because of the noise from your flat,
Your neighbours are always complaining,
Now what do you say about that?'

'I'll kick your teeth in,' said Grandma,
'I'll punch you 'ard in the eye,
I'll chuck you out of the window.'
'Oh yes?' said the man. 'You just try.

'You will have to turn down that rock music,
Stop the parties that go on all night,
Give up breeding rats, and machine gunning bats.'
But Gran said, 'Why? I knows me rights!

'I'm just a defenceless old lady,
In a very few years I'll be gone,
I 'ave just a few simple pleasures.
And bashing officials is one.'

So I kicked in his teeth while old Grandma
Gave him a belt in the eye,
Then we both chucked him out of the window,
And leant out and waved him goodbye.

DAVID ORME

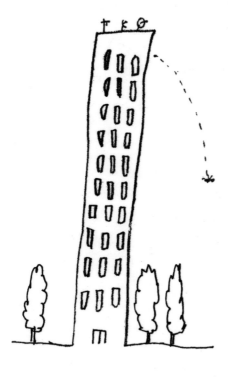

'Waiter, there's a thug in my salad!'

I'm an apple,
Used to hang round with a bunch of grapes.
The Hard Bunch, but they all ended up as winos.
Now I'm in the apple gang.
Wanna be in my gang?

For a start, we don't like oranges.
Any orange that gets in our way,
We squash! You should see them run!

Lemons? Yellow through and through,
Not as tough as me or you.

Lychees? Oh please!
They're a funny colour, and they're foreign.
Go back to Lychee Land.

Bananas? You must be bananas!
Fruit cakes all of them! Bender Boys.
Don't wanna get mixed up with that bunch.

Pineapple? What can you say?
I mean, zits or what!?
You could almost peel her skin.
She needs help badly!

180

Onion? What are you doing here?
Don't you know you don't belong?
Send for the doctors!
He's a total vegetable case!

Who does that leave?
Melony Melonbrain,
She's a pain, she's too fat,
Too soppy, too sweet
And she's soft in the head.
I think you're better off dead, my dear.

Pears? My older brother's a pear!
So pears are all right! All right?
In fact, he's so hard,
He'd have YOU for breakfast any day!

'Cos I'm a happy apple with all my apple friends.
If you wanna belong,
Don't be a lemon, or a stupid melon!
Just put on an apple skin and sing my apple song!
Apple! Apple! Apple! Oi! Oi! Oi!
Apple! Oi! Apple! Oi!
Apple! Apple! Apple!
Oi! Oi! Oi!

ANDREW FUSEK PETERS

Yobs

Me in the rain, my scooter broken down,
Fed up, pushing it, and these four lads
Block the pathway, jeering. Now, why's that?
No idea: for sure they don't know me.
I know them though (villages have eyes):
Petty vandals, go round daubing walls,
Snap the aerials off cars at night,
Wreck the children's playground, damage trees,
Tear the flowers up. Oh, I know them:
Know who's been expelled, in court. I know
Other things: I know who's unemployed,
Who come from broken homes, whose mother went,
Dumped him, four years old, to live with Gran.
I know who loiter now, unreachable,
By wasteland in the rainy winter dusk,
Who cry out 'Look at us!'
Not my affair.
I stand then, blocked, aggression's logan-stone
Poised, exquisite.
So, Who's leader? You,
Tall, in leather jacket, skull-adorned.
'Afternoon. You any good with these?
My baffle-pipe's gunged up, I've sheared the screw.'
Silence. Jacket boy considers me.
Thinking what? We've got a right one here?
Puzzled? Wary? I don't know. And then

'Hey, look, what you do . . .' 'He needs . . .' 'No, look . . .'
Hands in concert, octopoidal, blurring,
Strip, clean out, refit. I clear my throat,
Fumble in my pocket, find two pounds.
'Look, I'd like . . .' The leader, kneeling still,
Wipes his oily fingers, straightening,
Hesitates, then smiles and shakes his head.
The scooter starts first time. I ride away.

DAVID SUTTON

The Cake that
Makes You Scream

Underneath the icing,
Underneath the cream,
Underneath the marzipan
Is the cake that makes you scream.

It's filled with sticky spiders,
Slugs and earwigs too,
And swarms of tiny beetles
Swimming round in glue.

   Underneath the icing,
   Underneath the cream,
   Underneath the marzipan
   Is the cake that makes you scream.

It's filled with vampires' fingernails
And all their fingers too,
Crawling from the oozing sludge
Just to tickle you.

   Underneath the icing,
   Underneath the cream,
   Underneath the marzipan
   Is the cake that makes you scream.

It's filled with twisted nightmares
Where strawberries turn blue,
And fish's legs and donkey eggs
Growl and howl and moo.

Underneath the icing,
Underneath the cream,
Underneath the marzipan
Is the cake that makes you scream.

When you cut this curious cake
You don't know what you'll find;
Be careful or the slimey jam
Will climb inside your mind.

But even more important,
Be careful with the knife:
It'll try and slice your tongue out
Before you can take a bite.

Then you won't taste the icing
And you won't taste the cream,
And the marzipan will slobber out
In a sickening, shapeless scream.

DAVE WARD

Dream and Forgetting

My little girl is afraid to go to sleep.
Repeatedly she'll call me to her bed.
Perspiring gently when her slumber's deep
She trembles when I go to stroke her head.
She wakes so easily. Her eyes flick open,
She sits straight up, asks for a drink but can't
Get back to where she was. She can be woken
By a creaking floorboard. We know she wants
To only be with us, where we are, here.
She knows the hiding place we can't discover
And also what it is she cannot near.
She says goodnight as if it were for ever.
I sit in darkness, hear her breathing pulse
And slowly find I'm here and there at once.

GYŐZŐ FERENCZ
Translated by George Szirtes

Don't Be Scared

The dark is only a blanket
for the moon to put on her bed.

The dark is a private cinema
for the movie dreams in your head.

The dark is a little black dress
to show off the sequin stars.

The dark is the wooden hole
behind the strings of happy guitars.

The dark is a jeweller's velvet cloth
where children sleep like pearls.

The dark is a spool of film
to photograph boys and girls,

so smile in your sleep in the dark.
Don't be scared.

CAROL ANN DUFFY

Lullabye

(For Isabel)

No monsters are hiding under the bed
   I give you my word
The idea of vampires thirsting for blood
   Is plainly absurd.

There are no such things as ghosts I promise
   They're all in the mind
Headless horsemen, hobgoblins and aliens
   All nonsense you'll find.

You will not fall under a witch's spell
   You are not Snow White
Nor am I a handsome prince, but still
   A kiss, God bless, Good night.

ROGER MCGOUGH

Index of first lines

Index of author names

Acknowledgements

The publishers gratefully acknowledge the following permission to reproduce copyright material in this book.

'The Cane' from *Please Mrs Butler* by Allan Ahlberg (Kestrel, 1983) Copyright © Allan Ahlberg, 1983; 'Song of the Worms' and 'This is a Photograph of Me' from *Themes on a Journey* by Margaret Atwood. Reprinted by permission of Curtis Brown, Ltd; 'The Dream-Stealers' and 'The World's Worst Super-Villain' © David Bateman 2000; 'Entrails' by Connie Bensley, *Central Reservations*, Bloodaxe Books, 1990; 'Play No Ball' from *To Catch an Elephant, new and collected poems* by Gerard Benson, Smith-Doorstop 2002, by permission of the author; 'The Mobile Sting' by Gerard Benson. Reprinted by permission of the author; 'Don't Steal' by Ambrose Bierce from *Poems One Line Longer* ed. William Cole, 1973, published by Grossman Publishers, New York; 'The Last Witch in Nantwich' © Copyright John Burnside; 'Vlad' © Dave Calder 1997; 'Goodfellow' © Dave Calder 2001; 'Lord Lovelace'from *Collected Poems for Children* by Charles Causley (Macmillan). Reprinted by permission of David Higham Associates Ltd; 'Legend' from *Collected Poems* by Gillian Clarke. Reprinted by permission of Carcanet Press Ltd; 'The Girl Who Lit the First Fire' © Copyright Mandy Coe; 'The Art of Dying', winner of the first prize in the Salisbury Poets Open Poetry Competition. First published in *Starters 4* (Kick Start Poets 2001) © Copyright Mandy Coe; 'Confessions of a Failed Super-Villain', 'Stepmother' and 'The Evil Doctor Mucus Spleen' © Copyright Paul Cookson; 'Huff' and 'Cradle Song' by Wendy Cope. Reprinted with the author's permission; 'Alternative Endings to an Unwritten Ballad' from *Romantic Landscape: Poems by Paul Dehn* (Hamish Hamilton, 1952) Copyright © Paul Dehn 1952; 'A Ransom for a Cat' and 'Poem' © Copyright Peter Dixon; 'The Deserted Village' by Bertie Doherty from *Rusty Nails and Astronauts*, Wolfhound Press, 1999. Reprinted by permission of David Higham Associates Ltd; 'Don't be Scared' and 'Jamjar' from *The Oldest Girl in the World* by Carol Ann Duffy. Reprinted by permission of Faber and Faber; 'Buinneach Buí' © Ian Duhig; 'Big Wicked' reprinted by permission of A. P. Watt Ltd on behalf of Helen Dunmore; 'He and She' © Copyright Richard Edwards; 'Macavity: The Mystery Cat' from *Old Possum's Book of Practical Cats* by T. S. Eliot. Reprinted by permission of Faber and Faber; 'Charlotte O'Neil's Song' by Fiona Farrell. First published in *Cutting Out*, Auckland University Press, 1987; 'Dream and Forgetting' © Copyright Gyözö Ferencz; 'Nanny Neverley' and 'White Ones' © Copyright Philip Gross; 'Power' from *Underground* by Corrine Hales, Ahsahta Press, 1986. Reprinted by permission of the author; 'If People Disapprove of You' from *Leaving and Leaving You* (1999) by Sophie Hannah. Reprinted by permission of Carcanet Press Ltd; 'Something Made Me Do It' © David Harsent 2002; 'Max' reprinted by permission of PFD on behalf of John Hegley; 'Homework' © Copyright Stewart Henderson (2000) from *Who Left Grandad at the Chip Shop?* Published by Lion Books; 'It Wasn't Me' © Copyright Stewart Henderson 2001; 'Portrait of My Lover as a Teaspoon' © Copyright Selima Hill; 'The Third Fiddler's Story' © Copyright Siân Hughes; 'Haiku' © Copyright Mike Jubb; 'Mrs Dungeon Brae' © Copyright Jackie Kay; 'The Stones' by Brendan Kennelly, *A Time for Voices: Selected Poems 1960-1990*, Bloodaxe Books, 1990; 'The Hump' and 'Song of the Galley-slaves' by Rudyard Kipling. Reprinted by permission of A. P. Watt Ltd on behalf of The National Trust for Places of Historical Interest or Natural Beauty; 'Lazy Witch' from *A Song I Sang to You* by Myra Cohn Livingston. Copyright © 1965, 1959, 1968 by Myra Cohn Livingston. All rights renewed and reserved. Used by permission of Marian Reiner; 'The Huntsman' from *Selected and New Poems 1935-1989* by Edward Lowbury, published by the Hippopotamus